BEING GARDNER DOZOIS

BEING GARDNER DOZOIS

An Interview by Michael Swanwick

Old Earth Books
Baltimore • 2001

BEING GARDNER DOZOIS

Published by Old Earth Books
P.O. Box 19951
Baltimore. Maryland 21211

Book Design by Robert T. Garcia
Garcia Publishing Services
P.O. Box 1059
Woodstock, Illinois 60098
www.american-fantasy.com

10 9 8 7 6 5 4 3 2 1

ISBN: 1-882968-19-0

PRINTED IN THE UNITED STATES OF AMERICA
By Thomson-Shore
7300 West. Joy Road
Dexter, Michigan 48130-9701
www.tshore.com

For Susan Casper

BEING GARDNER DOZOIS

An Interview with Gardner Dozois

"It loomed huge and ugly on the intersection of the Street of Fools, the fitful yellow glow that streamed from its crescent windows straining vainly to pierce the moonless gloom of the planet's long night."

Your first story was "The Empty Man," which appeared in the September 1966 issue of Fred Pohl's WORLDS OF IF.

Gardner Dozois: God help us all.

You wrote that when you were seventeen.

Gardner Dozois: More or less. I may even have been a little younger when I actually wrote the story.

It came out when you were in the Army?

Gardner Dozois: I received notice that it had sold when I was in basic training, in fact. I got to revel in this for about a minute —Wow! I'm a *real writer*—and then some sergeant was kicking me in the ass and yelling obscenities, so the moment passed quickly. But I did get a couple of minutes to revel in it. The story appeared later that same year, but I was overseas in Germany by the time it actually appeared and I didn't receive a copy until some months later.

It's obviously a young work—

Gardner Dozois: Sucks! is the way we describe it in technical language.

But looking over it I was struck by what an elaborate background history you had created—the superman Jhon Charlton teamed with the alien doorkeeper Moros, the enigma of the Cube of Darkness on Milhar II, and so on...

Gardner Dozois: Well, this shows you that the sins of your youth always come back to haunt you. All I can say is that you should read some of the stories that *didn't* get into print. They're even worse. To understand *this* story, if anyone wants to make the effort (and I can't understand why anyone would bother), you have to realize that at that point of time, WORLDS OF IF magazine under Fred Pohl was running several series of interstellar spy stories of various sorts. There was the Retief series written by Keith Laumer, there was the Gree series that was written by C.C. MacApp. Poul Anderson's Dominic Flandry stories. Jack Vance's Demon Princes series, probably the best series of this kind ever done. Some of Zelazny's early stuff. Fred Saberhagen's Berserker series also functioned as this sort of thing, to a large extent. I had been impressed by these stories and that's why I produced this particular story, which is full of interstellar spy hugger-mugger and superpowered mutants and people who overthrow planet wide civilizations singlehandedly, and so on and so forth. I fairly rapidly outgrew this. It's probably just as well.

Looking at the story I thought it might have been conceived as part of a possible novel, but you say it was part of a series?

Gardner Dozois: No, I had not even thought of writing a novel at that point. Once again influenced by the fact that there were these linked series of intergalactic spy stories appearing in WORLDS OF IF magazine, I came up with the idea of writing several linked stories in this shared background. I did in fact write a semi-sequel to this particular story, which fortunately has been lost from human ken. And I wrote, I believe, one other story that shared a vague background with this story, but that also has been lost. Perhaps fortunately, Fred didn't buy any more of these, or my early career might have looked somewhat different than it ended up looking. I think I was safe, though. I am firmly convinced that the only reason that Fred bought *this* one in the first place was that he had painted himself into a corner at WORLDS OF IF magazine with his announced policy that he would publish a "first sale" story in every issue of the magazine. That meant that for every issue—and WORLDS OF IF was monthly at that point—he had to come up with a writer who had never sold anyplace before, and that's hard to do and find *good* stories every month at the same time. He did remarkably well, considering the constraints on him, but I am convinced that the only reason "The Empty Man" got into print was because there was nothing else that month in the slush pile that was not even *worse*. Which doesn't say much for what else was in the slush pile that month.

Your original title for this was "Prometheus Revisited."

Gardner Dozois: Yes, that's the original or pretentious version. Fred changed this to "The Empty Man," and in fact "The Empty Man" is a better title for it than "Prometheus Revisited."

I have to say that for an intergalactic spy story this is very dark. The hero is more a figure of contempt and pity than admiration, so obviously you were trying for something a little deeper even then.

Gardner Dozois: I guess this *was* a reaction to the stuff I was reading in the magazines at the time, the stuff that I was imitating in the first place. Not *much* of a reaction, perhaps, but even then you can see my tendencies toward bleak pretentiousness stirring and raising their ugly little heads here and there.

   This is the first story that I actually sold. It wasn't the first story I submitted, however. There was a process that went back beyond this sale for a couple of years. I had the usual writer's background of scribbling stories and incomplete story fragments in notebooks, little spiral notebooks in my case, Dime Store tablet type notebooks. Fortunately, all of this stuff has been lost, or somebody would no doubt dig it out at some point and humiliate me with it. But I went through the usual stages. I can remember writing a vast interplanetary epic in which someone is teleported to Mars in a manner suspiciously similar to that in the Edgar Rice Burroughs series, and has adventures and sword fights for several notebook tablets, until I got tired of writing it. I never did come up with an ending for that.

   I wrote another unfinished Dime Store tablet space epic that was strongly influenced by A. Merritt's *The Dwellers in the Mirage*, full of Very Tall People who had swords and lots of Aryan angst; everyone was blond, of course. About the same period, I wrote another fragmentary epic about Earthmen who find out that the Moon is honeycombed with tunnels left over from a former Lunar civilization, and they run into the Moonmen, who have been hiding down there since the Moon ceased to be habitable, and they all have lots of gun battles and sword-fights with each other in the tunnels—mostly because I couldn't think of anything *else* that they could do with each other—until I lost interest in the story and gave up on it.

Another early masterpiece, which I actually finished, was a long sword & sorcery story featuring a pair of heroes, one big and muscular, the other small and wily, who bore an amazing resemblance, suspiciously enough, to Fritz Leiber's Fafhrd and the Gray Mouser. I planned to write a whole series of stories about these characters, but never did, unfortunately for Fritz Leiber's lawyers, who probably could have used the work (actually, I think that I was safe enough, since I doubt very much that any magazine would have published them in the *first* place).

A little later on I filled up notebooks writing Henry Kuttner-like ironic short stories, except with no talent. None of these things ever got to the stage where I submitted them to magazines, and, if I had, they would have come right back, deservedly enough. But in fact, I never even thought about submitting stories at this point. The possibility never crossed my mind.

Somewhere about in the middle of high school, it occurred to me that one could indeed *submit* stories to science fiction magazines with the hope of actually getting them published. I believe this was suggested to me by the little disclaimer below the masthead in most science fiction magazines, where it says they are not responsible for unsolicited manuscripts. Which, if you think about it, means that they *do* get unsolicited manuscripts and that it would be possible therefore for *you* to send them an unsolicited manuscript, and perhaps they would buy it! Before I had made that mental leap, I'm not sure I realized where stories came from, or that it was possible for someone who had not been born to the purple or grown on a writer farm somewhere in New Jersey to actually submit a story for publication. But once I made this mental leap, I then began to actually submit stories to magazines. I submitted three or four stories over the next couple of years until I finally got my first personal response, a request for a rewrite on what would become "The Empty Man."

At least one of these stories, I believe it's the first story I ever actually submitted to a magazine, still exists in my papers at Temple University. If anyone is masochistic enough, they can go up there and look at it. It's about five pages long. A guy wakes up in a coffin, claws his way in panic out of the coffin and out of the grave, then stands dumbly around in the grave-yard for a couple of paragraphs until he realizes that he really *is* dead after all, then he sort of sighs and mumbles "Oh, shit," and slumps back into the grave. No plot, no ending. As you can see, I was already forging the literary habits of later years. FANTASTIC wisely rejected this beauty. I don't know the exact date on that, but probably it was sometime around my sophomore year of high school. Which would make it, I guess, about '62, somewhere in there at any rate.

A bit later, I did a story for F&SF's "unicorn and Univac" contest, which was a challenge to new writers to write a story based on a poem by Doris Pitkin Buck about a unicorn meeting a Univac. My entry didn't win, and is fortunately lost. Greg Benford won that contest, and you can still find *his* entry in print if you look for it, which goes to show you that winning isn't everything. Even today, decades later, a yellowing manu-script will occasionally show up in the slush pile that has a unicorn and a Univac in it for no particular reason, and you know it was an entry in that contest.

―――――――――

"Robinson had been driving for nearly two days, across Pennsylvania, up through the sooty barrens of New Jersey, pushing both the car and himself with despera-tion. Exhaustion had stopped him once in a small, rotting coast town, filled with disintegrating clapboard buildings and frightened pale faces peering from behind tight-closed shutters."

―――――――――

So you sold your first story, the Army got you, and four years later broke into print again. Your second published story was "Where No Sun Shines," which appeared in Damon Knight's *Orbit 6* in 1970.

Gardner Dozois: Yes, although it was not the second story that I actually *wrote* after that. The chronology is somewhat complicated in here, between the actual dates of composition and the dates of publication. While I was in the Army I produced several stories, some of which would eventually get into print, and most of which would not. Most of them are lost. I produced a couple of semi-sequels, as I said, to "The Empty Man." I produced another early comic thriller called "Point of Law," which still exists in rough draft at Temple University, God help us all. I produced a few other stories, and two short novels, one of which, called *No Place on Earth*, is lost. The other one was called *Danegeld* in the original, and, several years later, ended up being expanded by George Alec Effinger and myself into a determinedly mediocre novel called *Nightmare Blue*. Which actually did get published. I might have been tempted to do the same thing with the other short novel, which was no worse, but fortunately, it was lost in transit back to the States. However, I did write "Where No Sun Shines" toward the end of my army career. I had written a story called "A Dream at Noonday" beforehand, but it was published subsequently. At some time in here, during my army years, I produced a number of stories that did eventually get into print, but not until years later, like "Wires," "Conditioned Reflex," "In a Crooked Year." Just after my army days, while I was still living in Europe, about the same time I was writing "Horse of Air," I produced a story called "A Traveler in an Antique Land," which wasn't published until about twenty years later. Probably with a good deal of justification. But yes, "Where No Sun Shines" was my first *sale* after "The Empty Man." A long dry spell—well, not dry spell, since I *was* producing, but a long discouraging period later, where I had made my first sale and then everything I wrote later, when I *could* snatch time to write in the Army, was being rejected. This went on for years. So it was with a certain sense of relief that I did sell "Where No Sun Shines," because I was beginning to wonder if the first had been a fluke or a flash in the pan.

"Where No Sun Shines" is a dark story, both literally and figuratively, set mostly at night. I note one scene where Robinson is stopped at a police roadblock. There's a series of long paragraphs describing what Robinson is seeing and feeling and thinking, then abruptly there's a one-sentence paragraph: "He suddenly snapped the visa closed." You said you were trying for a cinematic effect there?

Gardner Dozois: Yeah, well, that's one of a number of effects I tried for. Probably with indifferent success. To reproduce a cinematic technique. You can do that with film quite easily, but it's much harder to do that on the printed page. I was trying to lull the reader and then startle him with a sudden movement. Make him *jump* when he gets to that line. How successfully this came off, I don't know, but that was the intent, to make the reader jerk, to give him a start.

The difficulties the country is going through are pretty much unspecified. There's a suggestion it's a black revolution, because at one point when the soldier sees a black man hiding, he immediately shoots him. Was this what you intended?

Gardner Dozois: Well, you have to understand that in the context of the times. The country had just gone through a number of major race riots—the Detroit riot, the Watts riot—and this story was a perhaps not particularly daring attempt to suggest that if things continued along these lines, we might actually end up in a full-scale race war, where black would be pitted against white. And, obviously, the whites are winning. The intention of the story is to show some white people functioning as an underground railroad to smuggle black people who would otherwise be exterminated to some sort of unspecified place where they would be safe, a place of freedom. And, of course, these people are intercepted and—these are the people in the van, not the narrator, who is just an observer—they're all killed.

I did at one point have notes, which still exist, in fact, for a novel in which the United States has been plunged into this sort of social situation, and there is a racial war going on. But I never did actually write that, I think because I realized that a good deal of it would have had to be written from the black perspective, and I didn't really trust my ability to convincingly write from the experience of a black ghetto dweller. So I gave up on that plan somewhere along the line.

In the opening sections of the story, the reader doesn't really know what's going on. Robinson, the narrator, is traveling by car and sleeping in gas stations with a tire iron in his hand. It's not until very near the end that you reveal there's a perfectly innocent reason for this. He's simply been stranded away from home when the airlines closed.

Gardner Dozois: Just someone who's been caught in the mechanism of social chaos. Which, at the time I was writing this story, seemed like a very real thing that could happen to you. Few people remember how close to the brink of total social chaos the United States seemed to be at that time. At least to my eyes, and I don't think I was alone in this perception, it didn't seem you would have to heighten this much more before systems began to fall apart completely and brutal repressions and reactions began to occur. And I think we *did* skirt fairly close to that, in fact. I find it interesting that this story is now becoming topical again. If the story didn't already exist, I could probably write it and sell it again now, and people would take it as a warning for the years ahead. There was a time in the seventies when this story began to look dated and no longer applicable to current social happenings, but I'm afraid that it's beginning to look more and more topical again as the years go by.

"I remember the sky, and the sun burning in the sky like a golden penny flicked into a deep blue pool, and the scuttling white clouds that changed into magic ships and whales and turreted castles as they drifted up across that bottomless ocean and swam the equally bottomless sea of my mind's eye. I remember the winds that skimmed the clouds, smoothing and rippling them into serene grandeur or boiling them into froth. I remember the same wind dipping low to caress the grass, making it sway and tremble, or whipping through the branches of the trees and making them sing with a wild, keening organ note. I remember the silence that was like a bronzen shout echoing among the hills."

Your next story was "A Dream at Noonday," in *Orbit 7* in 1970, which you said was written just before "Where No Sun Shines."

Gardner Dozois: Yes, several months before, I think. It was the first story that I was actually pleased with. Everything else I'd done to that point, I had serious misgivings about, even the published story. But "A Dream at Noonday" was the first story I wrote that I was ever *pleased* with, really, that I felt really functioned on a somewhat higher level than the stories I'd been turning out previously. So for me it represented a quantum jump in sophistication above what I had been turning out before. Making it at least the second quantum jump that I had gone through in my evolution up to this point, because at some point I stopped writing the interstellar spy stories and started writing more consciously arty anti-war type stories, several of which later got printed. But this was a quantum jump in sophistication above them.

Unusually for me—since I don't usually work this way—I wrote "A Dream at Noonday" all in one session of about two hours, in a sort of white heat. I sat down after work, in fact, in the newspaper office where I worked in the Army, and after everyone else went off, I just sat there at my typewriter and ripped this story off. It just came rushing out, with hardly any pre-planning at all. That's not the way I usually write. It's only happened a few times that I've produced a story that way, all in one sitting, as fast as I could type. So obviously there was something boiling just under the surface in the subconscious there, and the pressure reached a certain pitch and the story just forced its way out.

In this story, you alternate two lines, the "I remember" line, in past tense and the "It is raining" line in present tense. The memory passages are very rich and evocative where the present time with the protagonist lying in the mud in the rain dying, is very closely described and detached and cold.

Gardner Dozois: Yes, well, the idea in the other passages was to give a very cinematic effect, where everything was described in a very dispassionate, objective, cold way, as if you were seeing it through the eye of a camera. He doesn't *feel* anything about what he is seeing there. The emotion is all in the memory passages, the reminiscences. And perhaps to a certain extent that's because the narrator is, after all, dead.

I was about to ask you about that. All through the story, from the very beginning, he's dead throughout?

Gardner Dozois: Yes, he's dead from the very start of the story. From *before* the start of the story. "Marley was dead, to begin with."

And he doesn't know it yet.

Gardner Dozois: Well, whether he knows it or not is a question that I don't really get into. I did picture him as being dead from before the start of the story, however. The genesis of the story was a remark that I heard that in combat they break the dog tags in half when they can't immediately recover the body, and they jam the half of the dog tag between the teeth of the corpse so they can identify the body later when they have a chance to pick it up. When I heard that I had a very vivid sensory flash of having this dog tag jammed between *my* teeth, I could taste the cold metal and feel it wedging my teeth apart, and that led me into viewing what the whole experience would be like from the viewpoint of someone who was dead but still perceiving what was happening to him. That was at least one of the seeds of the story.

The memories just evolved as I wrote it. He had to have something he was thinking about while he was dead, after all, and I figured he would be picturing his past life. Dwelling on his past rather than on the moment itself, which was just being observed from his viewpoint in a very dispassionate way. As though the dead can only really live in their memories.

The first set of memories had a terrific description of trains, the boy thinking they run about hunting and mating in the night. Other images come in strongly of magic caves, of people snickering at him, and of sex, and then in the last memory before he enters the Army, in the train station, you

pulled all of these into one image when he's staring down the tunnel with the train approaching and thinks that it looks like a magic cave. I thought that was very crafty of you.

Gardner Dozois: Yeah, well, actually most of these images are from my life, in somewhat modified form on occasion, but basically from my own childhood. The images of the trains outside the windows were things I can remember thinking as a child. We lived near a freight yard when I was a young child and you could hear the freight trains slamming and booming most of the night. So that stuff was there. There's a bit of romanticizing in the middle, in that I did not have a girl I was interested in school who went out with some other guy, and I saw them in a car, and so forth. I just sort of made that up. Nevertheless the basic emotions, the basic images are from my own life. Including the moment in the train station, which is a very odd moment I've subsequently seen portrayed elsewhere, in a movie or two. When you leave home to go away into the Army, not knowing if you're going to come back or not, there's a odd poignancy to that, and that's what I was working with in that particular scene. And I had gone through that scene myself too, because of course by the time I wrote the story, I'd been in the Army for several years. So that's from the life as well.

One genesis of a minor point, one I always enjoyed, is that when he leaves on the train going to the army, he sees his old house, and he pictures himself looking out the window at himself going by on the train, that younger self not knowing that his older self is on the train. And indeed when I got on the train and left to go down to Boston to enter the Army, I *did* go by my old house and I did look out at it and have the same thought. Gave me the same kind of flash I later got from looking at Escher prints. So this material was all there to be used.

I think this is the first story where I actually tapped into personal material, rather than writing about intergalactic spies and people staggering around after the last battle on earth and things that I didn't really experience myself. I broke through into some personal material that had some significance for me, and was able to reshape it in a fictional context so that perhaps it had some impact for other people as well. So it was an important story for me.

It also expresses fairly well a sense I've always had of the *interconnectedness* of things. I've always had an intuition that if you could see the hidden and secret relationships of things, you'd find out that everything was *connected* to everything else. That's why all the symbols here reoccur and mix in complex cycles. It's as if here, for once, you can see the hidden connectors. Or maybe it's that *he's* seeing those connectors for the first time, with the special clear vision of the dead. I think I get that feeling across here as well as I've ever done it anywhere.

In the background of the memory line is a character named Denny, who grows up along with him and is loathsome, who wants to kill gooks like his old man, and parallels the protagonist. Then at the very end he dies too. It hasn't done him any good being loathsome.

Gardner Dozois: Denny was based on a real kid, or, rather, he's a combination of several different kids I knew when I was in school. I did indeed hear a kid boasting in school that his father had killed a lot of gooks in the Korean War and that he hoped the Vietnam War lasted long enough so that he could get into it and kill him some gooks too. Most of those people did end up going into the Army. Several of the kids from my school went into the Army at about the same time as I did and were briefly in basic training with me. I lost track of most of them, so I have no way of knowing whether the more warlike and gung-ho of them *did* wind up getting killed, but it's certainly not an unlikely scenario. Yeah, the irony was intended, the parallels were intended. It doesn't really matter whether you're gung-ho or reluctant. You're fed into the meat-grinder and you end up as sausage one way or the other. Regardless of what your intentions are.

As an aside, this was one of the earliest SF stories, in American SF, anyway, to deal with the thematic experience of the Vietnam War, especially from an anti-war slant. And it was written a couple of years before it was published, too, so I'm fairly proud of that.

"Sometimes when the weather is good I sit and look out over the city, fingers hooked through the mesh."

In *Orbit 8*, still in 1970, you had "Horse of Air." You did something very strange here, where you wrote it in three different voices alternating. Why did you do that?

Gardner Dozois: Yes, well, I was sort of flexing my literary muscles at this point. This was written after "Where No Sun Shines," which is a fairly straightforward narrative, and as most young artists are, I was very pretentious in those days. I wanted to show that I could pull off complex effects. I was also still suffering from an intense infatuation with Dylan Thomas and Thomas Wolfe, who had had a big effect on me while I was in the army. I was very hipped on complex structure and complex and difficult effects. I drew a complicated chart to keep what's happening in these three time segments straight, which I may still have up in Temple.

I haven't looked at the story for years so I'm a little shaky on this, but I *think* that what I wanted was that one voice always tells the objective truth, and the second voice fantasizes an exaggerated situation, and the third voice is capable of interpretation either way. I believe that is the way I set it up, although I'd have to look at the story again to be sure.

So it was a complex playing with point of view, basically.

Your unnamed narrator has no personal past, no personal memories, only memories of his class—we needed this, we did that. It's an extremely impersonalized voice, it seems.

Gardner Dozois: Well, that's probably because he was not so much a real character as a trope or a stylized voice. I was playing with an insight that the narrative voice of the character could lie, could say things that were not true. I was trying to show counterpoint to this by showing that an entirely different interpretation was possible to what the narrator was saying. Now my *own* opinion is that it's pretty clear from the text that this guy's just an old, broke pensioner sitting in a slum apartment and fantasizing grandiosely that he used to be rich and powerful but that they came and sealed him in and took all his money away from him. Perhaps because I was not looking at him as a sympathetic character, but more as a set of attitudes or postures, his actual individual past doesn't come into it. But I try to show this shift from one perspective—one way of looking at things—to the other throughout the story. Where he'll say one thing about the way things are, and then he'll be contradicted by the other voice. You can interpret it the other way around if you wish, that it's the voice of the plutocrat that's telling the truth and it's the other voice that is lying, I suppose it would work out just as well that way, but I think it's more likely that it's really the other way around.

At any rate, for its time it's a highly experimental story, for American SF, anyway, and I don't know where it would've gotten into print if Damon Knight had not bought it for *Orbit*. It probably *wouldn't* have gotten into print. And even for today it's somewhat weirder than is the norm for most short stories. Probably wouldn't sell in today's market, either. Mostly it was just me flexing my literary muscles and being as pretentious as possible. Although I did spend a lot of time carefully working out that this would all work out. So I wasn't *just* being pretentious. I was being pretentious but putting some work into it too.

"March 3
Started our shift underground today. Goodbye to the world again for a while I guess."

One more story came out in 1970, "The Sound of Muzak," which appeared in *Quark 1*, edited by Samuel R. Delany and Marilyn Hacker.

Gardner Dozois: Yes, "The Sound of Muzak" is second or third draft, drastically reshaped, of a story that I started in the Army. I had written an early draft of this which was only a few pages long, and then later I revised it and lengthened it. And then later still, when I was out of the Army but still living in Europe, I revised and lengthened it yet again, and it was this version I finally ended up selling to *Quark*. In its basic couple-of-pages format it was shamelessly and almost totally stolen from a story called "Game" by Donald Barthelme which I had found in a Judy Merrill anthology, which was about two men in a missile bunker whose job it was to shoot off the ICBMs, and they go slowly insane. I pretty much just stole this and rewrote it in the original version of the story. I later got somewhat embarrassed and added a good deal more stuff to make it different from the Barthelme story. In the third draft I included an entire new counterpoint plotline and—naturally—made the structure much more complex.

You have a terrifically scary line in here early on, "Furniture is more important than people." I was wondering if you had any comment on that since it seems to fit thematically into a lot of your work.

Gardner Dozois: I had been hired by the United Furniture Dealers of America to put this bit of propaganda into the story. Furniture sales all over America soared shortly after the story's release.

   Well, yeah, that is a motif that has cropped up in my fiction from time to time. The people who are alienated and affectless enough are more comfortable with things than dealing with other people. In fact with much of my writing, particularly my early writing, can be seen as a series of stories about failed attempts at communication in one form or another, probably culminating in my novel *Strangers*, where the entire plot revolves around the inability to communicate fundamental information about the nature of reality to each other.

You alternate between diary entries and present time, which is an effect you also used in "A Dream at Noonday," past and present alternating. Is there any particular significance to the diary's dates, March third through April sixteenth?

Gardner Dozois: Yeah, there was, although it's so rococo that I now realize that it's unfair to expect any reader to actually *grasp* this. But, as I say, I was more pretentious in those days. I believe the intention was that the dates go from the beginning of Lent to Easter, of course the implication being that at Easter the rock will be rolled away and they rise from the dead, except that they don't. So that was the rococo and arcane symbolism of the dates. In fact, I did actually sit down and carefully work them out at one point—although whether I did it correctly or not is anybody's guess, since math has never been my strong suit—but that was what I *intended* for the dates, at any rate.

Once again here, we have a story where my major concern was playing with the reliability of events or different perceptions of reality. Many of the people and the physical surroundings described in the story are people and surroundings that I had known in the Army. The basic thrust of the story is that they *think* that they have a choice, but it turns out that they never *did* have a choice to begin with. It's even bleaker than some of my other stories from the time, because they fight and argue about whether they should open the door and go back up to the surface without orders to do so, and even kill each other over it, and then it turns out at the end that they *couldn't* have opened the door in the first place. This has never been an option for them. The non-diary time line takes place after they have discovered this. They know now that there are no choices for them, and it's driven them all mad to one degree or another. Again, a very pretentious story, obviously by a young writer.

The mad Major in the middle of the story tells a little fable, where he says "Listen, let me tell you about security." He tells a wonderfully pointless story about being on guarding with a loaded pistol when a civilian tries to inspect the plane.

Gardner Dozois: Yes, indeed, this story was told to me almost verbatim by somebody who *was* trying to explain security to us at some point during my army career. Many of my stories, this one in particular, perhaps, were reactions to my being completely sick of the Army and the Army mentality. I wrote a number of them, and then realized that I would eventually have to get into some material other than just being displeased with the army mentality, so eventually I did move on. But this reaction did sort of dominate my early work.

I think there are some good parts to this story. It probably is not really successful overall.

Earlier you said your complaint was against the aesthetic of the military.

Gardner Dozois: Yes, this story's mostly understandable as my reaction against the aesthetic of the military, and as a long criticism of military mentality. The patriotic posters that I describe him looking at are real patriotic posters that I had to stare at at one time or another in my army career. I was being sort of indignant about this.

It's a pretty hopeless story. I mean, with many of my stories I can think up a rationalization why they're actually upbeat after all, but it's hard to think of such a rationalization for this story. Not only is it completely hopeless but it was hopeless *before* the action of the story actually begins. Everything has been worked out. All the drama takes place in the diary sections which have already happened. In the real-time of the story, everything is hopeless and the situation has already worked itself down to a bloody status quo from which they can go no further except by dying. So, a pretty bleak story on the whole.

"Did y'ever hear the one about the old man and the sea? Half a minute, lordling; stop and listen. It's a fine story, full of balance and point and social pith; short and direct. It's not mine. Mine are long and rambling and parenthetical and they corrode the moral fiber right out of a man. Come to think, I won't tell you that one after all. A man of my age has a right to prefer his own material, and let the critics be damned. I've a prejudice now for webs of my own weaving."

"A Special Kind of Morning" appeared in 1971 in Robert

Silverberg's *New Dimensions I*. I hope you're not offended, but I think it was another quantum jump ahead.

Gardner Dozois: Yes, I do think it was, in fact, another quantum jump ahead for me. This was an attempt to get into different sorts of material. I had published a number of stories by that point, three or four stories, I forget how many, and somebody said of me that I was the new anti-war poet of my generation or something. I became alarmed at being type-cast after only three or four stories as an anti-war writer, so I figured I had better write some different sorts of material.

I think the most notable thing about this story is the incredible elaboration of prose. It starts out with a snapper opening—"Have you ever heard the one about the old man and the sea?"—and it's very jazzy and playful. Why did you decide to do this kind of story?

Gardner Dozois: This is me flexing my literary muscles in a somewhat different way. Most of my career, in fact, can be seen as an attempt to bring under control and make useful a tendency toward very purple prose. I've fought all through my career to find a reasonable balance between purpleness and starking things out to the point where you can't get the sort of atmospheric effects that you can occasionally manage to pull off with purple prose. Ideally, what I've been shooting for, with indifferent success, is a prose which combines the best features of both, which is stark and simple and yet flexible enough to enable you to pull off somberly evocative and grandiloquent effects when they're called for in the text. Many of my stories are experiments with trying to work out this sort of hybrid.

I wrote the opening part in an elaborate pseudo-Shakespearian language which fit the mood of the opening framework, but which I found didn't really work in the narrative body of the story, so I pretty much dropped it there, or at least toned it down quite a bit, and ended up with something that was more like early period Zelazny or Delany than Shakespeare.

But why did I do it? I don't know. I was young, I was pretentious, I was an ambitious young writer, and it seemed neat. I suspect that most things in the literary world are done for these reasons, in spite of the elaborate rationales that writers and critics come up with for them after the fact.

There is a very high neatness quotient to this story. In particular, the technology of the war you set up, where on the one hand the Combine has biodeths and tacnukes and scatterfields and phasewalls and tanglefields and psychophysicists, and on the other side the Quaestors have bicycles and grunts walking up to heavily fortified installations with knives because none of the defenders know how to react to personalized death.

Gardner Dozois: Yes, I had a lot of fun playing with those things. I had been bitten by a book which nobody else at that particular point in science fiction seemed to be doing much with. That was *The Biological Time Bomb*, a non-fiction book which had all sorts of interesting things in it about the coming biological technology that would transform our lives, much the same way that nanotechnology is being talked about right at this moment in the field. So I worked in clones and people with no digestive tracts whose nourishment was beamed to them by broadcast matter, and various other things like that. Just to get a sense of far-future alienness, of how *different* these people were from us.

At one time I intended to use all this material in a novel. But it never did all come together and so "A Special Kind of Morning" is its only remaining artifact.

I think what I was doing here, and in a couple of subsequent stories that never got completed, was that I was groping towards a sort of proto-cyberpunk aesthetic. And I think that in this story I took it as far as I personally was able to, given my inputs and my capabilities and my personality. There are a couple of unfinished stories where I tried to take it further and grope my way into something like *Neuromancer*, but I didn't have the stuff to do this, and in fact was unable to complete those stories. It took Bill Gibson coming along sometime later and a few other people to take this to where I could dimly see it ought to be taken. I didn't have the legs to do it myself.

I do think that this story can be considered as a dim progenitor of cyberpunk or as a distant ancestral figure. And in fact a couple of cyberpunk writers have mentioned that they did in fact read this story early on and were impressed by it. I'm certainly not trying to say that all of cyberpunk sprang from this story like Athena from the brow of Zeus, but I think it was an early indication that people were beginning to bend their thoughts towards the creation of a different aesthetic way of looking at the future. Eventually somebody better qualified than I to do so did break into that territory. But I think that this story was at least a signpost pointing in the proper direction.

You did something really amazing here, which is that you wrote the entire story backward. You begin with the climax of the war, then you go a step back to how they'd been fighting the war, then you go back to show you what kind of society they were opposing, and then finally you tell who the people in the story are and where they came from. And at that point the story is almost over.

Gardner Dozois: I've always liked to play with complicated structures. In fact, one of the big differences between my later work and my earlier work is that in my later work I'm less interested in playing with complicated structures and more interested in "a plain tale plainly told," to use a beloved critical term. But in my early stories, yes, there's no doubt that the

more complicated I could make the structure, the more interesting I found the story. Sometimes I made the structure so
complicated that the story is practically incomprehensible! In
this particular instance, I think I managed to balance it out with
an interesting enough objective story that the reader is pro-
pelled from one end of the story to the other. At least I hope that
the reader is.

One of the big things I was trying to get across in this story
was a perception that people in the future would be radically
different from us. From our current perspective, this does not
seem like a wildly innovative thing to have come up with, nor
was I the only person or even the first person to have come up
with it. But if you read the science fiction of the time, it was a
perception that was often lacking: that the people of the future
would be really *different* from us, more alien from us than most
science fiction writers' aliens are. So I enjoyed playing with
that.

Some of my innovations here are so wildly unlikely that I
don't think I've even seen them stolen anywhere else. Like the
broadcast matter replacing the need for a digestive system. Or
the entire army that packs down into a little cube that you throw
into the back of a truck somewhere. But I had a lot of fun playing with that sort of thing. This is in a way the apotheosis of the
interstellar spy stories that I had been writing in an earlier
incarnation. If, at the time I was writing them, I had had any
real talent or knowledge of the world or ability, they might have
come out something like this. It is, perhaps significantly, the
last interstellar story I wrote, with the exception of my novel
Strangers. I believe all the rest of my stories have been set in
Earthly milieus. So perhaps I did as much as I thought could be
done with the material—at least, what I thought *I* could do with
the material, always a different thing.

I at one time contracted to write a novel version of this
story, and found, when I sat down to do it, that I couldn't,
because I had already said everything I wanted to say with this

material in the compass of this novella, and I couldn't see any way to expand it into a novel that didn't involve outright padding of the most shameless variety. And while I wouldn't necessarily be averse to doing this shameless padding for the money, it's more a matter of I *couldn't* do it, because I've never been able to make myself write anything at any length that I wasn't interested in. So it's not so much a matter of virtue that I didn't pad it out into a novel, as it was that I was unable to work up enough enthusiasm to be able to pad it out.

There's a lot of tricky stuff in here. For example the climax of the human story is when the narrator goes to kill the null and finds he cannot, for he accepts the null as human. At which point the war is basically over for him. As a result of this moment of kindness, he survives, but the narrator then immediately mocks the idea that there's any significance to this.

Gardner Dozois: One of the philosophical linchpins of the story is the idea which the narrator expresses somewhere in here. Ah, here it is. "The universe doesn't care one way or the other; only people do. The universe doesn't give a damn. It isn't out to get you, and it isn't going to help you either. You're on your own. We make our own heavens and hells and can't pass the buck." Rather a simple philosophical statement, but one that was important to me at the time.

Your main character finds it liberating. He's able to look back after all these years, dying in the gutter after a life filled with a great deal of pain, the war not the least of it, and he finds it cheers him up immensely.

Gardner Dozois: I found it bleakly liberating myself. I remember once when I was living in an apartment with some other expatriates in Germany, I went to visit England for a couple of weeks. On my way back to the apartment from England, I was working over in my mind what probably had happened in my absence. You must realize that I knew these people and their interrelationships extremely well. I spent the entire trolley ride to the house working out in my mind every possible scenario of their interrelationships that could have occurred in my absence. And when I got back to the apartment, I found they were all down with the measles! Which possibility had not even *occurred* to me to factor into my calculations.

This actually came as a great relief to me, because I realized then that whoever was running the universe, it wasn't *me*, that the universe was much smarter than I was. I could never outguess it. It could always take me by surprise. So therefore I wasn't God, *I wasn't* in charge, whoever was, if anyone was, and I did find this a liberating thought. You can never outguess the universe. It always has a surprise in store for you. It's almost pointless to try.

For all that this is a lot of fun—you could make a great war game out of this if you wished—this is still in disguise yet another anti-war story. In spite of the fact the protagonists are facing a nearly unqualified evil, the war is so awful they come close to simply giving up.

Gardner Dozois: My feelings toward the whole thing didn't change. They just became a little more subtly expressed. The problem with writing an anti-war story, as somebody points out somewhere, is that you might as well write an anti-glacier story. The sad thing is that I think there probably *will* continue to be war in the future, as long as the human species survives. Of course, it's problematical how long that's going to be.

Unlike Jerry Pournelle and the rest of the boys, I don't take comfort in the idea that there's always going to be war. I've always thought that the tone of the title of those anthologies was: *There Will Be War, Thank God—What a Relief, We Were*

Worried There for a Minute! But with all the best will in the world I think there *will* always be war, or deadly conflict of some kind, as long as human beings manage to survive, and manage to remain human. I must admit that I find very few of the pacifist utopian scenarios at all convincing. I know human beings better than that. We're a pretty vicious lot when you come right down to it.

In the frame the old storyteller is talking to the young lordling who's just gotten laid for the first time and is feeling pretty good. Is this just me, or is there an implication here that this is probably the old guy's last morning alive?

Gardner Dozois: You could certainly read it like that. I think that would be a valid interpretation. On the other hand, I'm not sure I actually had that in mind when I was writing the story. I think I saw him as continuing, where he would go on like this morning after morning. Where for the young person to whom he's telling this story, it's a significant one-time encounter, for him it's probably quite different.

This is probably the story that did the most to establish my early reputation. And I knew at the time that I should write a lot more stories like this, but somehow I could never bring myself to get interested enough in anything else of this sort to actually produce it and finish it. If I *had* been able to turn out a lot more stories—and, in particular, novels—of this sort, I have no doubt that my subsequent career would have looked very different. I would probably have ended up making a lot more money than I'm making today, because there's clearly a niche here that's waiting for someone to fill it, and even was waiting for someone to fill it in 1971. It's sort of one step beyond early Delany. Delany himself did not go on to take this step, going on to write more opaque fictions instead. You had to wait until about '77, when Varley appeared, for someone to take another step in that direction, and then of course Bruce Sterling and Bill Gibson and the cyberpunks later on took it even further. But that line was waiting to be exploited by somebody. I had positioned myself early to exploit it, but through a failure of nerve or imagination or creative energy or whatever, did not actually manage to go on to exploit that niche. So, of course, some other little animals crawled out of the underbrush and radiated out ecologically to fill the niche later on. So I missed my chance there.

"I find that death is not like they said it would be in the manual. The sun was too bright and too hot and when it rained it was real rain that soaked your clothes and skin and made you shiver in spastic paroxysms. And it was real blood that mixed with the rain and with your bitter sweat and flowed down into your eye-sockets, blurring your vision so that you pawed frantically at your eyes with your good hand, trying to bring the fading grey world back into focus."

In December of 1971, there was a small story called "Wires," which appeared in a special Guilford issue of Ted White's FANTASTIC.

Gardner Dozois: Yes, Guilford was a science fiction workshop that was run in Jay Haldeman's house—Jack C. Haldeman—in the Guilford section of Baltimore. It was the first unofficial science fiction workshop that I was involved in. I had been at a Milford workshop before Guilford started, and, in fact, Guilford sort of evolved out of the Milford, in that there were a bunch of us Young Turk writers who all knew each other, and a couple of us had been to a Milford, and we decided to have a Milford-type workshop of our own. So for a few years in the early 70s, we would all meet at Jay Haldeman's house every few months and have a workshop. Charter members included Joe Haldeman, Jay Haldeman, myself, George Alec Effinger, Jack Dann, Ted White. On various occasions other writers like Bob Thurston and Tom Monteleone attended.

One weekend Ted announced at the end of the workshop that he was going to buy several stories that had been in the workshop for the special Guilford issue of AMAZING or FAN-TASTIC. And he did so. And bought a lot of mostly mediocre stories that had been in the workshop, and ran this special Guilford issue. I was in there, Jay was in there, George Alec Effinger was in there, I think maybe Thurston—I'd have to go back and find an issue and look.

"Wires" was a story I'd written much earlier, I believe just after I'd written "In a Crooked Year" and "Conditioned Reflex." It's clearly thematically pretty much the same as those stories in its concerns. I think it was a little more sophisticatedly executed than either of those, but it's still fundamentally conveying the same message, and belongs to roughly the same period in my career. Of course it was a trunk story for many years and finally found its way into print via the Guilford issue of that magazine.

It begins, "I find that death is not like they said it would be in the manual." In many ways it reads like an earlier draft of "A Dream at Noonday."

Gardner Dozois: Similar in tone in some ways I think to "The Sound of Muzak," although perhaps a little jazzier. I haven't reread the story in years so it's a little difficult to bring to mind. I believe however that it was actually written *after* "A Dream at Noonday." I think "A Dream at Noonday" is the superior story, so if it *is* another take of "A Dream at Noonday," then I did it right the first time and shouldn't have bothered going on to try a variant of it again.

It has an odd tense change here.

Gardner Dozois: If you went back to 1969 and tracked down the boy that I was and asked him why there was a tense change there, I'm sure he would have a perfectly good explanation for it. However over the intervening years I've forgotten what it is. I haven't actually looked at this for years. Let me see that.

I think the reason for the tense change is that the opening five or six pages is him philosophizing about his death after the fact, and then when the tense change and the space break comes, from then on that's him describing his actual death as it's occurring. That's only a guess though.

"—He crouched near the command vehicle and listened to the nervous thrub-dub of his heart. The grass tickled his skin, like tiny scratching spearpoints. Idly he wrapped a finger around an emerald blade of grass, wrenched it out of the ground, and was instantly sorry; he had already killed too many things today."

In 1972, David Gerrold's *Generation*, a new writer's anthology, contained "Conditioned Reflex," which I believe was the opening section of the work that included "The Sound of Muzak," and "In a Crooked Year."

Gardner Dozois: As you say, this is an earlier story that waited several years to actually get into print. I suppose that if I were a more noble intellectual sort, I would have suppressed all these old trunk stories. But I usually needed the money, and so over the years I have sold just about all of my completed trunk stories. They have all come out, sometimes to my embarrassment, but usually to total indifference and lack of response from the audience, which is perhaps just as well. This is a very naïve young man's story, burning with youthful idealism, about how the last two groups of soldiers in the world batter at each other until they're all dead and humanity is extinct. Well-meaning, but very naïve.

This is about the last battle, but there is no explanation of what it's about or how it came about or even if it matters or not.

Gardner Dozois: This was conscious even at the time. That was part of the point of the story, that it didn't matter what the war was about. To some extent I still feel this way today. I mean, when we go into a nuclear spasm war scenario and we destroy all life on Earth ten times over, I don't think it's going to matter all that much what our *reasons* were for doing so. Certainly it won't matter to the intelligent cockroaches or whatever creatures radiate to take over our ecological niches after the fact. So yeah, that was in there. That was part of the point even at the time. I was naïve, but I wasn't *that* naïve.

You had the officer trying to stop the firing at the end—I believe this is the only time you ever had an officer try to achieve something worthwhile.

Gardner Dozois: I think the implication there was that things were so horrific that even the *officers* realized that things had gone too far, but that once the process had gone on to that extent, there was no way you could stop it even if you wanted to. Which again is a point that remains valid even today, in the face of the enormous computerized defense systems that we have. Certainly it's as valid now as it was in the sixties. The only difference is that in the sixties people used to *worry* about it and write stories about it, and now, when it's in some ways even more valid, they've put it out of their minds and don't want to even think about it any more. Past a certain point it doesn't matter whether you want to fight a spasm conflict or not; you're going to fight it whether you want to or not. Just as in "A Dream at Noonday," the kid who wanted to enthusiastically kill gooks and the kid who was dragged into it reluctantly both end up dead. It doesn't matter what their individual inclinations are, once you get fed into the meat grinder, you're sausage. Even if you do have good intentions.

"Each day, Mason would stand with his hammer and kill cows."

"A Kingdom by the Sea" came out in 1972, in Damon Knight's *Orbit 10*. Did you actually go to a slaughterhouse for your research?

Gardner Dozois: No, I didn't. I sort of researched, but I sort of cheated, too. My total research consisted of having a long conversation one evening in the house of a friend in Greenwich Village with somebody who *had* worked in a slaughterhouse and had observed people hitting cows over the head with a hammer. From that one long conversation, I took all of the authentic detail about working in an old fashioned slaughterhouse. I believe they don't slaughter cows in this fashion any more, but they still did at the time I wrote this story. I think they have a mechanically operated hammer or lever of some sort that crashes down now, and they don't actually hit the cow with a sledge hammer.

Several people have complimented me on the research, and asked if I did indeed work in a slaughterhouse. I take that as a compliment to the degree of authenticity I was able to con people into believing here, since I never did work in a slaughter-house. I have, however, worked in jobs that, as the narrator says, are unpleasant enough that the people have to keep them as far away from them as possible while they're doing them, so perhaps some of that seeped through.

There's also a lot of tough description of blue collar life in here. Mason's entire history, drifting about, ending up caught, the life he leads, are very convincing.

Gardner Dozois: Well, after all, I was a working class kid who grew up next door to a factory town. My father was a factory worker who worked in a chemical factory, and most of his friends were blue-collar factory worker types. So I have observed that milieu enough that perhaps some authenticity came through. It's interesting to me that very little is written about those type of people in science fiction, even today. Even the cyberpunks writing about their mean streets and their - backroom lowlifes don't actually get into blue-collar factory industrial worker type people much.

There are very few writers in science fiction who come from a working class background. Almost everyone, even people like Lucius Shepard who write consistently about the lowlife types in back streets, come from a middle class or upper class background. Other than myself, I think the only other actual working class boy in science fiction is Howard Waldrop, who also came from working class parents. Almost everybody else is middle class or up. And it's too bad, because there's a lot of stuff about that class that would make interesting material if it was translated into fiction. You don't see it very much.

Structurally, the story opens with the sentence of Mason killing cows. Then there's your description of his job, and what it's like and how he lives, and it ends with that same

sentence again. That's an interesting thing to do. It brings the story to a dead stop for a second.

Gardner Dozois: Of course the whole point of the story is that he is in a dead stop and doesn't realize it until the end. This is one of two or three stories in my career where the nub of it came from a dream, which was essentially the climactic flash at the end. I then rationalized the rest of the structure backwards to create a story in which this could happen.

It's again one of my tricky stories in that you could read it in one of two ways with equal validity as far as what's on the page is concerned. If you read it as the story of someone who encounters a telepathic cow, then it is indeed science fiction, albeit science fiction of a somewhat silly sort. I think the more likely reading—which I insist is not the real or true reading, but rather my reading of the story—is that this is a man slowly having a mental breakdown under the appalling circumstances of his life, and he is holding off from himself a realization of how completely dead-ended and hopeless his life is by creating the psychotic break type fantasy of being contacted by this pure, elegant female spirit who is going to redeem and apotheosize him. Then at the end this realization that his life actually is hopeless and dead-ended comes crashing through from his undermind and he destroys the fantasy. And at that point pretty much destroys his life. That is at least my own interpretation, or my favorite interpretation: that when the hammer comes crashing down on Lilith at the end, he is actually destroying himself. That is the end of his life. He may continue on, eating fig newtons and burned frozen pizza for another twenty years, but in fact everything is significantly over at that point.

So in this regard it's similar to "The Sound of Muzak," in that there never really was any way for him to get out of this situation. He merely fantasizes that there is a way out of this situation, and then at the end the fantasy falls through. He sees through it and is psychically destroyed. Now, of course, this is a rather dramatic young man's way of looking at it, since if you look at it objectively there probably *are* ways that a man in this situation could better his life or get out of this situation he's in. But that isn't what I was interested in getting across. And, in fact, to be fair to my younger self there are many, many people who really *do* live lives of quiet desperation that are no better than the life that the person is living in the story.

The visions of the pure female spirit are very science fiction kind of images, and there's an implication here that these kinds of fantasies are not really much use to somebody in such a hard place, that they're lies and delusions.

Gardner Dozois: You'll notice at the end that just before Lilith shows up and is a cow, he is desperately trying to imagine what she would be like when she comes, and he is unable to imagine this. Which is the place I think where the fantasy fails for him. He really cannot imagine what this kind of transcendence would be like; it is beyond him to imagine this. He says, "She would arrive any second. He could not imagine how she would come or from where. He could not imagine what would happen to him, to them. He tried to imagine her arrival, but his mind, having only Disney, sci-fi and religion to work with, could only picture an ethereally beautiful woman made of stained glass descending from the sky in a column of golden light while organ music roared. He wasn't sure if she would have wings."

Now obviously his imagination has failed him completely. He can't reach transcendence because he can't *imagine* transcendence. If he *could* imagine transcendence, then he would have imagination enough to look at his life and realize it is a dead end and do something to get out of it or to alter it or to make it better. But he obviously cannot.

Similarly, there's a point at the beginning of this story where he's criticizing what the landscape that he's watching through the bus window looks like. There's a similar failure of imagination there that hints at the failure to come at the end, where he knows that he doesn't like the landscape he's looking at, a landscape of gas stations and factories and dilapidated, fenced-in yards and so forth, and he knows there ought to be some better way for it to look, some better way for it to *be*, but he can't think what that could be. Because he doesn't have the *words*, he doesn't have the concepts. And that, I think, is the problem with many people who are stuck in this sort of situation. They've never been exposed to the words or the concepts that would help to liberate them, and so they don't have them as part of their arsenal of tools to use to manipulate the world.

Of course, you can see this as tremendously autobiographical, since I was a poor kid in a factory town environment, and manipulated my way out of it because I *did* have the concepts and the words. I'd been exposed to them through reading science fiction books, in fact! Whereas my friends and neighbors and relatives did not. So I suppose after I'm dead, if anybody still cares anything about my work, some psychiatrically-minded critic will have fun with that particular insight.

You have frequent tense changes between past and present tense, and I can't readily decipher the pattern. Why did you do this?

Gardner Dozois: I know that there *was* a rationale for the structure, because at that time, when I did a lot of complicated structure, I was very careful to always follow some sort of symmetrical rule. But it's been so many years that I'm not really sure off the top of my head what the rule was here.

The problem with explaining a lot of this stuff is that to a large extent I've always been an intuitive writer. I will do something because it *feels* like that's the way that it ought to work. Then I have to bring my pitiful intellect to bear after the fact to explain why I did this instead of that, and it's not always easy to come up with a convincing rationale for it that will explain it in left brain terms.

I worked very closely with Damon Knight on this story, going over it line by line, and that was a learning experience for me, valuable when I started editing on my own.

"The world solidified."

The next story, "The Man Who Waved Hello," came out also in 1972, in Terry Carr's *Universe 2*. It starts out with Harry Bradley lying naked on the floor, coming down from an egomorphic drug—ten thousand years subjective experience as somebody else, which you immediately forget when you wake up.

Gardner Dozois: I still think that's a drug that would be immensely popular today if someone would come up with it.

In a way that opening is a deliberate distraction from what the story's setting out to do. Because it really isn't about the egomorphic drug at all.

Gardner Dozois: No, I've always been a sneaky little devil. There's always been a lot of stage misdirection in my stories. There are several stories where I will leave the facts in front of your eyes nakedly, but distract you from the significance of them by shooting off guns and whistles and doing other things. I like to do this because I like to play fair with the reader, and yet fool him at the same time. So that is indeed a deliberate stage misdirection in the beginning.

Also, however, it picks out the fact that the actual life that he's leading is incredibly mundane and food-processed and bland and plastic and boring and hideous and so forth. And one of his ways of escaping from it is, of course, into the drug, but he also has *other* ways of escaping from it. Which takes us into the meat, as it were, of the story.

You've created an economic system there in which it doesn't matter how much money you make, you can never pull ahead or feel secure.

Gardner Dozois: Do we have a different system now? If so, I'm not aware of it.

This is even worse because if they do catch him and he loses his job, even if he isn't thrown in jail, then tomorrow he's on the street. He doesn't even have a month's grace time.

Gardner Dozois: That's pretty much true of myself today as well, so perhaps this is not so much science fiction as we'd like to think. I think it's true of many people today that if something went suddenly and catastrophically wrong, a month or two later they'd be out on a hot air vent. That's certainly true of me. I have no economic cushion. If I lost my job or became incapacitated tomorrow we'd be out on a hot air vent a month from now. So although I didn't think of myself as a prophet at the time when I was writing that, perhaps it's not so far off the mark. Actually, at the time I was writing it I was so poor that it didn't much matter, although I wasn't on a hot air vent, admittedly.

This was a story that primarily started off as a joke. I had gotten the idea of someone who would call somebody up on a viewphone and expose himself. I thought this was a pretty funny concept, and then sat down to write a story that would rationalize this taking place, provide some motive and setting for this to take place in.

I was originally supposed to write this as a collaboration with Joe Haldeman. We were sitting around in my decaying apartment on East 10th Street in New York when something he said prompted me to come up with the joke about someone exposing himself over a viewphone. I said, Well, why don't we write a story about that? and he said, Oh all right. So I sat down and wrote the first draft of the story—actually it was a few weeks later when I was visiting Joe and Gay where they used to live in Washington, in College Park. I sat down in their living room after they'd gone to bed and wrote the first few pages of this story, but when I showed it to Joe he thought it was such a trivial piece of nonsense that he didn't want his name associated with it. So I went on and wrote it by myself rather than giving it to him to work on.

Sort of foreshadowing "A Change in the Weather."

Gardner Dozois: There's nothing new under the sun.

Some lessons must be relearned in every generation.

Gardner Dozois: So I did indeed go ahead and write the trivial bit of fluff and sell it, and to my knowledge it has never been reprinted since. It's one of my more obscure stories. But it did earn me some grocery money, so I don't disown it particularly. I do feel rather proud of the fact that almost certainly sometime in the future, when and if viewphones become more common and widespread, it will occur to somebody sometime to call somebody up and expose himself and hang up. And when he does, I will be triumphantly vindicated as a major prophet of science fiction.

At the climax of the story when he actually makes the

obscene phone call, there's a carefully described moment of contact with the woman. "She stared at him in shock—but there was also a quick flicker of fascination behind her eyes, and something else. Recognition? Longing? Love?" Is this response on her part just in his head or does it imply that she's caught in this same kind of wretched, horrible world and welcomes the contact?

Gardner Dozois: Of course, there's no way to really know on the paper whether it's in his head or not, since it's all seen through his own subjective vision. My own interpretation at the time was that this did indeed mean that she also was caught in some hideous grey plastic trap of her own. And that even though this was disgusting and nauseating and perverted, at least it was something different, something that broke through the usual routine. So that there was a moment of contact at this level.

I was probably impressed strongly on some subconscious level by a statement that I can vaguely remember, I think it was by Theodore Sturgeon, that even a punch in the mouth is communication. I've worked variants of this idea into various of my stories.

"On his way down to the dying ocean, Kagan came across some cops looting a grocery store."

Your next story, still in 1972, was "King Harvest," which appeared in Silverberg's *New Dimensions 2*. It starts out with Kagan's encounter with the policemen. He's chased away, and then they're the only people he sees until the end of the story. It's interesting that having established there are other people yet alive, you then dismiss them. It's

harder to pull a story along with one man alone and nobody for him to interact with or have gun battles with.

Gardner Dozois: I suspect that I am more likely to write a story in which someone staggers despairingly around by himself for forty pages than to write a story in which the same person staggers around having lots of gun battles. That's just an example of my writing personality, I guess. I was hinting that there might be survivors, or at least that there would be people who were willing to *try* desperately to survive. But that the vast majority of the people, particularly the protagonist, were not going to survive.

I think there's a tendency when you write about the end of the world or ecological catastrophe, to visualize yourself as one of the survivors—you know, *you'd* make it through. I never found this particularly convincing, because if there is such a catastrophe, I don't think *I'm* going to make it through. Perhaps this reflects my own lack of confidence in my ability to survive after the collapse of civilization, in that the viewpoint character here is one who *doesn't* make it, and watches the rest of them roar off and maybe survive. Although again, there's no concrete evidence that the tough cops with the riot guns and the oxygen masks are going to survive either. They're just making more of a fuss about it before they succumb, perhaps. That's left up in the air.

The story was basically an attempt to reconcile two irreconcilable aesthetic states. To present a story where there was no hope for the character at all and despair was total...and yet somehow show a grain of hope, spiritually, at the same time. That's a pretty difficult thing to do, and whether I pulled it off here I can't say. Basically, the story is Kagan working through the way he feels about dying, and about this vast catastrophe, to the point where he *himself* feels some sort of peace. He's at peace with himself to some degree by the end. Of course he dies anyway, but then it was clear that he was going to die from the very beginning of the story.

You may argue, as I believe someone did argue, that it's *false* hope that he feels at the end, a false peace. Maybe it is, maybe it isn't. It depends on how the rest of the scenario works out in the larger world. But he at least has staggered through his own dark night of the soul and by the end has come to terms with himself. He realizes that he was guilty by implication in the catastrophe, as indeed we all are, but he realizes that he wasn't *particularly* guilty as an individual, actively guilty. It was more a sin of omission than commission. And has pretty much come to terms with that by the time he actually dies.

I think this story dances right on the edge of me being satisfied with it. There are things about it I like. On the other hand, I think I wrote it in too heavy a way. It takes too long. Physically speaking, the *paragraphs* are too long. If I were going to rewrite the story now, I would go back and break up the paragraphs into much shorter, more quickly-moving paragraphs. Since there are huge blocks of text there, paragraphs that take up practically the whole page. Which felt right to me at the time, since I was writing it in a very stately, slow-moving style deliberately, but I get impatient with it re-reading it. I might cut some of the description of the ruined city out too, since there's quite a bit of it. But that's all hindsight.

This story is chockablock with crucifixion imagery. He sees the image of Christ crucified, of course, but there's also the girl's body in an awkward position that suggests crucifixion, and he wraps her up in a shroud and carries her in a manner that recalls the Passion of Christ. This is obviously deliberate.

Gardner Dozois: Yes, well, it was, of course. One thing I work with in the story is a see-sawing of perception. The events remain the same throughout, but the way he *interprets* the events changes. So it's a struggle between two modes of perception, and he finally ends up in one. Which is the somewhat more reconciled, hopeful—perhaps falsely hopeful—mode that he ends up perceiving things through at the end. But throughout there is a see-sawing of his perception of the same events.

This is particularly noticeable in the sequence with the dead girl, where, seen from one mode of perception, this is deeply affecting, and his wrapping her up in the shroud and trying to give some dignity to her death after the fact is a deeply meaningful act. Yet seen from the *other* perception, it's ludicrous and pointless and perhaps even blackly funny that he wraps up her body in an awning and puts her inside a butcher's counter. He sees it from *both* of these perspectives at the same time, flashing back and forth between them. He finally comes to rest in one by the time the story's over.

"Dawn was just beginning to color the sky. She huddled inside the small bathroom—door closed, bolt slid and locked—sitting on the toilet lid and hugging her knees. Her head was tilted and hung down, chin almost to breast, and her eyes were nearly closed. She had wrapped her hands around her ankles. Her fingers were turning white. There was no noise in the empty apartment, not even the scurry of a cockroach. She had stopped crying hours ago."

"Machines of Loving Grace" came out in 1972 in Damon Knight's *Orbit 11*, and it has something new for you—a female protagonist. Why did you decide on a female protagonist for this particular story?

Gardner Dozois: I don't have any really good answer to that question. As to why I was using male protagonists before, I suspect that, like many young writers, my early stories featured glamorized versions of myself, staggering around doing one thing or another. In other words they're very self-centered stories. I think this is true of most young writers to one extent or another. The instinct is to first play with versions of yourself, and then later on you get interested in putting other sorts of characters into the stories. So that's probably as close to an answer as I'll come up with.

In the opening section, you have a meticulously described bathroom—really, one of the great depressing rooms of literature—with cracking plaster and a shower curtain with yellow swans and so on. Was this a real place?

Gardner Dozois: Yes, that is a fairly accurate description of the apartment that I was living in on East Tenth Street in New York City when I wrote the story. For verisimilitude, I actually sat in the bathroom, on the closed toilet seat, while I wrote the scene that took place in the bathroom in the story. So the description is from the life, except for the package of vaginal suppositories, which was poetic license. Everything else was real, all of it.

That must have made you feel rather strange, considering that what your protagonist was doing in the bathroom was slitting her wrists.

Gardner Dozois: I had a lot of fun imagining how the blood would look as it hit the bathtub and washed down the drain. The view from the window that she describes is also a somewhat poetically dressed up version of what I could really see out the bathroom window while I was writing the story.

This was done in four sections: The suicide from her point of view, the resurrection from the viewpoint of the technicians, a lecture from the viewpoint of the baffled doctor,

and finally a short return to the protagonist. This is all in service of brevity, I take it?

Gardner Dozois: It wasn't an idea that would stand a lot of exposition. It's a sort of one-jab idea. I wanted to get in a quick jab to the belly and then get out again. The genesis of this story was a remark that a friend of mine made to me once that sat in my mind for a number of years. A young woman I knew who had serious emotional problems—she'd been in and out of institutions and periodically tried to commit suicide with one degree of seriousness or another. She once said to me that an attempt to commit suicide was not really an attempt to destroy yourself, but rather an attempt to resist forces that were trying to change you into someone you didn't want to be. That stuck in my mind, and for some reason, I forget the exact stimuli, a few years later I got to thinking about that, and produced this story, in which there's a high-tech rationale for someone being able to commit suicide over and over again.

This is sometimes seen as a very depressing story in that the protagonist kills herself over and over again. I have an argument I use to counter this—which argument has in the past made George Martin for one laugh like a hyena—that this is actually an *upbeat* and optimistic story. Because the point is that the young woman is still *resisting* the forces that are trying to grind her down into hopeless conformity, by struggling against them with the only weapon she has: continuing to kill herself. So therefore she's still fighting and resisting and struggling against the forces of oppression, and *therefore* it's fundamentally an optimistic story. If I had ended the story where she gave up, and said she would do what they told her, and didn't kill herself anymore, *then* it would be a downbeat, despairing story. Because she gave up.

This argument usually gets a laugh from the people I'm telling it to, but I think there is a tiny trace of validity there.

This is an extremely short story. The description of the suicide takes up three pages, and at that point you're halfway through the story. You must have gone through a great deal of trouble keeping the length down.

Gardner Dozois: I think it's a better story for being short. I wanted to do it in the minimum amount of space, because I thought it would be more powerful that way. If I had spent a lot more time describing the set-up, I think that it would enable you to pick holes logically in the social set set-up, and that wasn't what the story was set up to do. The story was designed only to deliver that one-jab philosophic point, and the social surround that enabled her to keep on killing herself over and over again was sketched in only enough so that it would be convincing *while* you were reading the story. I could easily have stretched things out quite a lot by handling the other section as a moment to moment narration from the viewpoint of one of the technicians. You know, him coming to work and putting down his lunch pail and thinking about his dog and his wife and scratching his ass and walking around and thinking about how the whole technological set-up works. I could have padded this out quite a bit. But that would have given you more time to think about the social set-up and pick holes in the plot logic. So instead I sketched it in, in the minimum amount of time, what in a *film* could be done in one five-second take. If you could bring in the underlying conceptual material somehow, you could do it in a very short take, where the light goes on in the board, the technician looks up and says, "Christ it's *her* again. Why does she do this?" and the other guy says, "Fuck her. She's nuts," and they throw the switch. You'd be out of the scene in about three seconds. That's basically all you need. In and out, very fast.

So, yeah, I tried to make this as tight as possible. I think it helps the story to be that tight. You certainly can't *dwell* on it and have it hold up. It's almost a surrealistic story, in that the science fiction element is there to make you *accept* it as reality just long enough so that you can get the philosophical boot in. But if you start to *think* about it, and analyze it, and parse it out logically, the social set-up they have here is not very likely. It's meant to be *just* likely enough to get you to swallow the story, so the little time-capsule of philosophical content can go off in your gut afterwards. It wouldn't have held up under a long treatment, it would have come apart like wet toilet-paper.

"Machines of Loving Grace" was the story with the smallest time lapse between my writing the story and my selling it. I wrote the story one night in my apartment, and a day or two days later I took the story along with me to the SFWA Friday night Nebula Award party in New York. Damon Knight was there. He read it while sitting on a couch in the SFWA suite, and bought it on the spot. So it was only a day or two days from completion of the story to sale. I don't think I ever bested that record.

"Southward, behind him, are years of success. They stretch back in an unbroken, creamy line, like the cloud cover beneath the airplane: solid, smooth-textured, no rough spots, no ragged edges. He can number the years. Sitting in the turning silence, he holds them securely in his mind and leafs through them ruminatively, examining them, running them through his hands, sniffing some with satisfaction, stuffing others into his mouth to taste again."

From one of your better known stories we pass on to what is perhaps your least known story, "Flying."

Gardner Dozois: Well, perhaps not unjustly my least known published story.

This came out in 1973 in the Autumn/Winter issue of EDGE, subtitled SF DIRECTIONS, which Bruce McAllister was guest-editing?

Gardner Dozois: Yes, McAllister was guest-editing an issue of an established literary little magazine. This may be one of the most rare compendiums of the seventies. I don't even have a copy of it anymore. I know there were quite a few other science fiction writers of the time who contributed little bits of this and that to it.

I wrote this story at the 1970 Clarion. I was unofficially guest teaching with Damon and Kate. Damon Knight and Kate Wilhelm were down there for two weeks as the official instructors and I as a wandering Young Turk of the time dropped in down there and unofficially helped them teach for a couple of weeks. One night I wanted to dash off something of my own so it could be put into the workshop for fairness' sake, so I sat down in the cafeteria and dashed this off. I thought of it more as a prose poem than an actual narrative, although there is a thin narrative thread throughout. Mostly it was a transmogrified use of thoughts that I had flying out there, and that I had jotted down.

So I did write this and put it into the workshop the next day. Where it was *slaughtered*, I might add, particularly by Damon Knight, who hated it, and cut it to ribbons. Probably not undeservedly. It's not by any means a significant story. It's a pretentious bit of fluff. I think it has some merits if you look at it as a prose poem or a little conceit rather than an actual story, but certainly it's nothing to set the world on fire.

In it the protagonist, thinking back on his past, sniffs the years and puts some in his mouth—the old man in "A Special Kind of Morning" uses this phrase too, talks of stuffing experiences in one's mouth.

Gardner Dozois: I guess this shows I'm an oral personality type. No doubt a Freudian psychologist would have a good deal to say about this. And indeed, if you look around the squalor of this apartment, which I haven't cleaned for a couple of days here, you'll see that I'm probably an oral type. Although there is an anal streak to me way down deep which emerges every so often. When I'm doing accounts for anthologies and so forth, I find that I actually rather enjoy adding small amounts of figures together. I think that my anthologizing ability is rather an anal ability. I often compare anthologizing to Japanese rock gardening, where you say that white rock will look aesthetically pleasing in juxtaposition with this red rock. This is pretty much the way I come up with the contents of a reprint anthology. So I guess there is an anal streak down there somewhere. But as anybody who's seen me will testify, I'm primarily an oral personality. So I guess this is why my protagonists are stuffing memories in their mouths. At least they're not stuffing them up their nose. This would give the psychologists something different to worry about—the nasal personality.

In the story the narrator is thinking of things and then through a prose trick he becomes the airplane and falls— he's turned into metaphor.

Gardner Dozois: It was all metaphor. As I say, more of a prose poem than an actual story. I thought it was all right for a little conceit that I had ripped off in an hour in the cafeteria, but clearly it's not a major work.

"One day the aliens landed, just as everyone always said they would. They fell out of a guileless blue sky and into the middle of a clear, cold November day, four of them, four alien ships drifting down like the snow that had been threatening to fall all week."

In 1973 you had "Chains of the Sea," which appeared in *Chains of the Sea*, a collection of three original novellas edited by Robert Silverberg. Obviously this is built around the child, Tommy—was Tommy actually you?

Gardner Dozois: "Chains of the Sea" again dips into my childhood experiences. There is a fairly high autobiographical content there. Many of the things in the story did happen to me. Many of them *didn't* happen to me as well, of course, and many of them happened but in somewhat different form, that being, I guess, artistic license.

The story was originally commissioned by Robert Silverberg, to be published as one of three novellas in a book of stories by young writers. The other two were George Alec Effinger and Gordon Eklund. This is what I produced for the book. I'd wanted to make use of some childhood experiences and fantasies and perceptions, and while thinking about what to write for the Silverberg book, I suddenly saw a way that I could use this material, working it in with another idea I'd had, about how perhaps aliens wouldn't be as impressed with the concept of Man, the paragon of Animals, the Master of Creation, as we ourselves obviously were.

The title comes from Dylan Thomas or from Bob Dylan?

Gardner Dozois: Well, it sort of cheats. Word for word it comes from Bob Dylan: "The chains of the sea have been shattered in the night, and have fallen to the bottom of the ocean." But I also had in mind a poem by Dylan Thomas. I was quite taken by Dylan Thomas in those days. The line I had in mind was, "Time held me green and dying, though I sang in my chains like the sea." However, "Chains Like the Sea" didn't have the right ring to it so I ended up using "Chains of the Sea."

You can tell I was impressed by Dylan Thomas by how many of my stories have stolen titles from him. For instance, "Where No Sun Shines" is from a Dylan Thomas poem. So is "In a Crooked Year." And, of course, if you wink at it a little bit, "Chains of the Sea."

You have two lines alternating, one of Tommy Nolan and his life, and the other an omniscient overview which begins "One day the aliens came just as everyone had said they would." That seems a very storybook opening, as if you were sitting a child down on your knee and telling a fairy tale.

Gardner Dozois: Well, I wanted a unique way for the aliens to land. I was tired of them landing in the way they always landed in stories. So I made up a rather strange process for them to manifest themselves through rather than just coming down in ships. I have subsequently seen a couple of things in other writers' work which I believe were influenced by this.

There is a very arch, ironic tone, blackly satirical, to the omniscient overview sections, so maybe that's where the "storybook" feeling you're talking about comes from. I consider much of what happens in those sections to be blackly humorous—there's a furious black anger there as well, but also a lot of bitter humor that mostly is carried by the *tone* of the prose itself. This is probably the closest I ever came to writing satire of the savage early-Vonnegut sort.

I notice here a technique you use elsewhere, which is that you hide the Other People in plain sight for a time. Tommy makes reference to them, but it seems to be of a piece with his imaginative life, being a puddle-jumping machine and so on.

Gardner Dozois: I did often as a child, which probably says

something bad about me psychologically, fantasize myself as a machine or a vehicle. This puddle jumper that he's being on the way to school was a game I actually *did* play as a little kid. I would fantasize myself as this vehicle, which would chug along and then be able to spring way up in the air. If you're going to write from the viewpoint of an alienated child, obviously it helps to have *been* an alienated child. My advice for other writers who would like to attempt this: "Kids, don't try this at home!"

This story was set in Maine, you said once?

Gardner Dozois: Well, officially it's set in the little strip of coastal New Hampshire in between Massachusetts and Maine. But much of the landscape that's described is pretty much the landscape of where I grew up in coastal Massachusetts. Many of the things that are described are things that I knew when I was a kid. However it could be set most anyplace along the New England coast north of Boston, and it wouldn't make that much real difference. I deliberately left it vague, although if I were writing the story these days, I'd probably pin the location down to a specific town.

In the alien line you have the AI and its counterpart intelligences secretly ruling the world, rather than the humans who only think they do. It seems ironic that the human race has been conquered even before the aliens arrive.

Gardner Dozois: Well there were lots of little ironies here. The whole basic idea for the story was that aliens would come down and people would try to contact them and they would ignore the people and talk to the ones who were *really* running the place instead, which was certainly an ironic idea. I myself found that idea amusing in a bleak sort of way. So there is a bleak satirical humor here that shows up in several places.

I believe I was one of the first people to actually use an

artificial intelligence as a character in fiction, especially one referred to by the term AI; later they began showing up all over. There may have been other people who used AIs in stories first, but there weren't too many of them.

In one scene Tommy invents a story of a dragon being hunted by a Navy warship. He tries to let the dragon off the hook by having him escape across the land, but his friends tell him he can't do that, the dragon has to die because it's chained to the sea. You have a little fable in the middle pointing up the message of the story.

Gardner Dozois: That's sort of a bonus. For those of you who didn't buy the *Cliff Notes* version of this story. The Official Author's Message. This is Tommy sensing that he is doomed and trying to think up more cheerful alternatives. But he can't really place any credence in them. Because at some deeper level he *knows* that he is doomed and that he is *not* going to escape. And in fact he does not.

Even without the fact that the aliens are winding down the world and everyone is going to die—in some ways that's the least of Tommy's problems. He has a really bad life. They send him to a psychiatrist as a punishment and the psychiatrist diligently tries to make him worse and even more alienated.

Gardner Dozois: I have never been real sympathetic to psychiatry, perhaps for the reason that when I was in school we indeed *were* threatened periodically with the school psychiatrist. Occasionally the more distanced members of the class would actually be sent to the school psychiatrist with the implicit and sometimes not so implicit threat that they would clap us away in the loony bin somewhere if we didn't shape up. I remember having the school psychiatrist poring over the drawings I'd made in art class of Romans fighting with swords and of dinosaurs and telling me about all the repressed psychoses and neuroses and everything that this showed because I had people fighting with swords. Phallic symbols, you know, and the fighting demonstrated repressed hostility. So this sort of pop psychiatric stuff definitely was used as a weapon at that level at that time. There was also a sense that it was used as a social weapon, to help keep the working-class in their place. So perhaps it's not surprising that some of this came through. Although the psychiatrist is wildly exaggerated in the story. There's a question as to whether he actually is this distorted, or this is just Tommy's prejudiced perception of him.

There's a possible reading of this story that the aliens don't land at all, that this is just a fantasy Tommy spins as he descends into madness, especially in the last scene where he's been cut off from his family, cut off from friends, the psychiatrist is working on him, and he sits at his desk staring straight ahead, frozen. Even his fantasies have deserted him.

Gardner Dozois: Well, yes indeed, this is a game that I've always enjoyed playing and many of my stories are open to this interpretation. I usually, when I'm playing the game well, try to provide two equally valid interpretations. You could read the story as objectively happening in the fictional reality or you can read it as him going insane and having his fantasies darken down toward termination. Or you could read it as both. This stuff could be objectively happening to the world *and* he could be going insane and having his fantasies darken down to termination at the same time. I don't think there's anything you can actually put your finger on in the text that favors one interpretation more than the other. The fact that the alien line is couched as omniscient description would lean a little toward the objective definition, but you could also argue that this was

just a fantasy that Tommy was having. So you could play the
game here. It's a little blurrier in some of my other stories.

"The valley was aflame behind him. Behind him, his
companions burned and smouldered like fitful tallow
candles, and the flames of their burning stained the
night sky with dancing scarlet and molten gold, ghostly
chemical green and white-hot blue, blotting out the
stars."

**"In a Crooked Year" came out in 1973 in Roger Elwood's
Ten Tomorrows. This has the soldier wandering about after
the final battle described in "Conditioned Reflex." I notice
it alternates between first and third person—I'm wandering around alone, as opposed to He is the last man on Earth.**

Gardner Dozois: Once again, I had some idea there that the two
voices would *comment* on each other. It was again a switching
of perception from one mode to another. I think—without looking at the story to be sure—that one voice was giving a subjective version of the facts that the other voice was reporting in a
slightly different form. But I'd have to go back and look at the
story to know if that's what I was after. This is a story written at
the height of my youthful pretentiousness, and I'm not sure it's
really worth talking about. It's an amazingly pretentious story,
crammed with overwriting and purple prose and ludicrous psychological and philosophical posturing of one kind or another. I
believe he even shakes his fist at the sky and rails at God at one
point, chastens the Almighty for stacking the deck of the world
unfairly against him. Dreadful. So I'm not sure what of value
can be said about this story, except that it was a very young

man's story, written when I was very young and pretentious and full of angst and ambition and seething hormonal changes of one sort or another. It's certainly not a successful story. It may have one or two good lines or images embedded *in it*, but as a *story* it's pretty much a dead loss.

This is a trunk story that sat around for years until I became well-enough known to con somebody into buying it. It was originally part of an even more pretentious story. "Conditioned Reflex" was the opening chapter. In "Conditioned Reflex" the last battle on Earth is fought, and then in the *rest* of the story, which became "In a Crooked Year," the last survivor of the last battle staggers around melodramatically railing against the fates until he finally dies himself. I finally realized that it was too pretentious even for *me* to have "Conditioned Reflex" as part of this, and so trimmed off "Conditioned Reflex" and sold it as a separate story. In fact, at one point I remember trying, as a masterpiece of incomprehensible pretension, to smoosh "Conditioned Reflex," "In a Crooked Year," and an early version of "The Sound of Muzak" all together, working "The Sound of Muzak" in as a counterpoint line to the other stories. I even have a faint memory of trying to cram "Wires" in there too, as yet another counterpoint line. But this made up into such an incredible tangled incomprehensible ball of roaring adjectives and shameless pretension and philosophical mishmash that even *I* was ashamed of it and gave up the idea of trying to make it work, and instead took it to pieces again and sold the pieces as trunk stories over the years.

You're pretty cagy about the narrator's name. At one point he says, "I cannot remember my name. It began with a D or a B. It could have been a G." Which, for one thing, is obviously a joke on your own name.

Gardner Dozois: Yes, that's true. Wasn't I clever? This is what happens when you allow nineteen-year-olds to write stories.

Why is it that so few of your protagonists have names, and when they do have names tend toward vague, noncommittal names like John or Kagan or Tommy?

Gardner Dozois: From some pretentious intellectual source along the way, I picked up the idea that the less you characterized the protagonist as an individual, the more you made him an Everyman, and the easier it would be for the reader to identify himself as the person in the situation. Which is why many of the characters from the early stories don't even have names. I think this was supposed to facilitate your identifying yourself with the character in the story. Similarly, I didn't use identifiable backgrounds, specific backgrounds that existed in the real world, in many of the stories. They all take place in a sort of stock background that could be any number of places rather than specifically taking place in Chicago or El Paso or something. I later changed my mind about this, and began to write stories that did indeed take place in specific environments in the real world, places that actually exist, rather than places I made up. And I later tried to make my characters actual individuals rather than open-ended symbols that the reader could read themselves into. Just one of the many ways a writer's work evolves over his lifetime, if he holds up long enough.

Something that's interesting in light of your later work is that near the end the protagonist sacrifices a bird in order to bring back the sun in winter. What was meant by this? Was this just part of his psychic breakdown, or is he reverting to a simpler mental state?

Gardner Dozois: I think it shows him reverting to a primitivism where you attempt to control the universe by mystical, supernatural means. In a way I'm getting at the same thing here that Lucius Shepard gets at in a much more sophisticated way later in "R&R," where he has a soldier in a constant life-threatening situation trying to *control* that situation in his favor by many small supernatural manipulations. He always goes to the same bar, and he always plays the same song, and he always wears the same shoes, and so on. It's a way that people instinctively try to control situations where they really *have* no control. I think people need to feel that they *do* have control even when they don't, and this is why they so constantly think up systems that make it *appear* that they have control. They need to be able to fool themselves that there *is* some way that they are contributing to their own fate, in order to keep functioning. Whereas in truth, the *reality* is that whether he goes to the same bar or not, or puts on his lucky shirt or not, he really has no control over the situation. These are just things he does to keep himself going, because there seems to be a human need to be able to tell yourself you do have control, when, in fact, you usually do not. Mason does this, throughout "A Kingdom by the Sea." The same thing is true of the protagonist of "In a Crooked Year." He is making up rituals intuitively, to try to alter the situation, when in fact the situation cannot be altered and is not altered. So that's sort of where that comes from. I think most magic is of this instinctive, intuitive kind.

As an aside, when I was young I did know a kid who was fond of doing things like this, getting small animals and birds and nailing them to a board and torturing them messily. He was caught at it several times. God knows what became of him. He's probably working for the Pentagon by now.

This kind of instinctive magic is something I do play with a lot in my stories, because I think it's a part of life. I do it myself. We all look for omens. We all have little superstitious rituals and fetishistic things that we do. We do them to give ourselves the illusion that we can control the universe in our favor when, in fact, we probably cannot.

"He can feel them in the air around him, swimming through the walls, the ceiling, the floor, always just out of sight. What they are he doesn't know, but they are there."

Your next story is "The Last Day of July," which came out in 1973 in *New Dimensions 3*, edited by Robert Silverberg. John has come to an isolated house because he's undergoing a nervous breakdown. He appears to be a writer; is he an avatar of yourself?

Gardner Dozois: John probably is an avatar of myself in some ways. The house and grounds that I describe closely in this story actually do exist, or did exist some twenty-odd years ago. It's a house in Milford, Pennsylvania, where I lived for a period of some months. The genesis of this story probably comes from my spending many long days there alone and feeling alienated from myself and my surroundings, an effect isolation tends to produce. In the story, it's simply taken to an extreme, where the character becomes more and more attenuated from reality, ever more isolated, as if he's a sail of some sort and there's a steady pressure of solar wind on him. Eventually he's just blown right out of reality—or maybe that's too dramatic; eventually he just *fades* away from reality. Drifts away. And I suppose that in my self-dramatizing moments of loneliness, that's what I felt was happening to me. Of course it *didn't* actually happen, but the feeling that it was, or could, is probably the major seed of that story.

The story has a strong sense of the aliveness of things. The

**house is described as a magical thing, where sundogs wink
at him from windows, and he steps into a circle of magic
stones.**

Gardner Dozois: That sense of everything being charged with
spirits and magical significance was quite deliberately put in
there. In fact, one of the major pleasures I took in the story was
engineering those impressions. They are all things that I have
felt to one degree or other myself. I think that at heart I am
probably a primitive animist, in that there's some part of me—
intuitively, down deep—that believes that everything is alive
and charged with spirit. Perhaps this goes back to when I was
a little kid and listening to the freight trains boom in the freight-
yard and picturing them as great magic animals. Perhaps its my
Celtic heritage, I don't know. But I *do* often get a feeling—that
I don't take seriously with the left-brain intellectual part of my
personality—that everything is alive and swimming with numinous spirits, and so forth.

    Most of the feelings that John has in the house and grounds
are feelings that I myself had there, although in less intense
fashion, little fancies of emotion that scurry across your mind.
He *feels* them much more deeply, but obviously I had to feel
something similar in the first place in order to conjure them
onto the page. The story is full of things like the scene in the
kitchen in the morning, where the mist is surrounding the
house, and he's lighting the gas oven for warmth, and he fancies there's water lapping up against the wall. Then, of course,
the mist burns off and there is no water. Again that sort of flip-
flopping of perception, seeing things both magically *and*
rationally at the same time, is one of the things I was after.

**In light of that, then, the visions he had which drove him to
the house, of apocalyptic London, would be the same
visions you wrote about in "A Traveler in an Antique
Land," would they not?**

Gardner Dozois: You have to realize that while "A Traveler in an Antique Land" was published almost a decade later, maybe even longer, than this story, it had been written several years before. So "A Traveler in an Antique Land" was part of *my* mental furniture, even though it wasn't part of anybody else's mental furniture at that point. Probably there are references back to that story, even though this story was published years before.

I could have had him stumbling around in any locale, talking about how the visions had driven him to isolation, but it happened that I myself had returned from England not many years before, so that was a place I had on my mind. So it was natural that I used London for the place he was staggering around in. But he could have been staggering around in Chicago just as easily.

John proceeds to sink down below the surface of the world. At one time he has a vision of a woman naked beside him in a bed and also a whole roomful of people, interesting people with glittering eyes, who beckon to him to join them. But he moves on from them. What was going on there?

Gardner Dozois: I saw this as the world trying to hold on to him, hold him on this ghostly atavistic level. Obviously if he had stayed, he would have become one of these shoals of drifting ghosts who are floating through the house, and, by extension, floating through the world. He would have remained on that level. But in fact he sinks *through* that level and beyond it to something else. So he doesn't end up as a ghost haunting that house.

In fact, because I was living in an isolated house in the woods, I often fancied that there *were* ghosts of all sorts swimming about me. It was kind of a spooky place in some ways. Frequently you would hear odd noises and footsteps that couldn't be accounted for. So that all got worked into the texture of the story.

In meditative yoga there's a point where you begin to break through into higher realms, and the gods appear and offer to make you a god, to share in their pleasure and sex and so on. But you have to give up your quest, and the wise man is urged to spurn them. Were you thinking of this when you wrote that scene?

Gardner Dozois: It's possible that I was. I had read several mystical texts by then. I was also influenced by the belief that after death you experience a period where you *believe* that you are still alive. Various things happen to you, and you face increasing hostility, and things go wrong, and eventually you *realize* that you are dead. Then you can go on. That may have been mixed up in there somewhere. That's all in *The Tibetan Book of the Dead*, although I forget what that state is called. No doubt it could be dug up out of research materials.

This is another story which can be read two ways. It could literally be happening, he could be one of the seeds the universe plants so that a new universe might bloom with life elsewhere, or he could be simply going mad, losing all contact with the world in a more metaphoric sense. But at the end, you have the concrete imagery of the world he lands in, with the rich, dark earth under his fingernails. "The earth is fertile. There will be a crop." That seems to weight it in favor of the literal, optimistic reading.

Gardner Dozois: I think I leaned a little in that direction myself in this particular case, although as usual I like to play the game that other interpretations are equally valid. I emotionally tend toward him having *actually* gone through into the other universe in this case. I weigh toward the literal interpretation in this particular case, where in the case of "A Kingdom by the Sea," for example, I tend to weigh things toward the non-literal interpretation.

Where did the title come from?

Gardner Dozois: There's kind of a lame joke there. It's a line from a song called The Cuckoo is a Pretty Bird: "The cuckoo is a pretty bird/He sings as he flies/But he never never cuckoos/Until the last day of July." This is one of those pieces of information that not only have absolutely no value, but probably *shouldn't* be known if people are going to have any respect for your work at all.

That's always been a story that I've liked. It was a story that has been almost completely ignored. It attracted no attention when it appeared and has attracted no attention subsequently, either. Although Michael Bishop once told me he had been impressed by that story, that it was one of his favorite stories. Other than that, I don't think anyone has noticed it at all.

"Ben Jacobs was on his way back to Skowhegan when he found the abandoned car. It was parked on a lonely stretch of secondary road between North Anion and Madison, skewed diagonally over the shoulder."

Your next story was "Flash Point," which came out in *Orbit 13*, edited by Damon Knight. This was your spontaneous combustion story. One thing I found interesting was that you provided several incompatible causes for whatever it is that's happening. There's a group of Satan-worshippers who may have called up this evil upon the world, there's a factory at the edge of town which is releasing *something*, there's the inherent meanness of the human spirit. At one point I worked it out, and there's something like five different explanations for what's going on, buried in there.

Gardner Dozois: The Satan-worshippers are more an example
of the decay of the times and the failing of human values than
they are there to suggest a cause for the spontaneous combustion. I may have been less subtle than you think here, since I
always thought that the primary cause of the plague, in the
objective world at any rate, was the factory doing biological warfare research. Although there is a sort of metaphysical,
metaphorical or spiritual level on which it is suggested that it is
in some way also a result of the breakdown of communication
and human values and warmth between individuals in our world.

I don't think that it ever occurred to me that the Satanists
were conjuring up demons who were then causing these spontaneous combustions to happen. I suppose, though, that that's
as valid an interpretation as any.

**You also come very close to suggestion that there's some-
thing fundamentally wrong with human beings, and that
given just a little snap of control, this is what they revert to:
to Satan worship and spontaneous cruelty and such. Even
the protagonist, Ben Jacobs, who is a decent, humane man,
feels this downward pull.**

Gardner Dozois: As I said, while the objective cause of the
plague probably would be the biological warfare station, there
is a whole metaphorical level here in the story where he himself wrestles with losing control and slipping into this sort of
barbarous behavior that underlies human nature and is covered
up with a thin veneer. In that sense I think you're probably correct. Metaphorically at least, the story suggests that when we
lose control of our own humanity and abandon it, then other
forces from within and without rush to the fore and take over
our lives. Bursting into flames at that point and burning into
ashes is just a metaphor for this process of abandonment and
destruction. Although it is one of those stories where I try to
have it on two levels at once. The metaphysical meaning and

the metaphor is there at the same time as the fact that I envisioned an actual physical cause for them bursting into flames. It all ties in together. So I hope, anyway.

On a less exalted level, I notice that this is set in Skowhegan, the "home of the largest sculpted wooden Indian in the world."

Gardner Dozois: Yes, well, there is a real Skowhegan, Maine and it really does advertise itself as the home of the largest sculpted wooden Indian in the world. I've been there a couple of times. I take a sly pleasure in setting stories in obscure real physical locations. I suppose that's an in-joke to some extent.

I did take a trip to Skowhegan with an old army buddy in the early seventies. After I got back from this trip I was walking down Second Avenue or Third Avenue in New York and lines of dialog in the sort of voices that I had heard there began to speak themselves in my mind. Local color was very important to this story, in that I knew where I wanted to set it and the kinds of people that would be in it. I just had to find something for them to be doing, basically, a reason for the story to exist in the first place.

I also wanted to show that isolation is not really a defense against this sort of spiritual corruption, and that in fact in some ways isolation itself may be a vehicle for expressing this spiritual corruption.

There's a technique I used here, I don't know how successfully it comes across, which is a technique that I adapted from a series of stories that I admired a lot as a young would-be writer, but which I doubt that you've even heard of, called the Mad Friend stories by G.C. Edmondson. Which was a series that he ran in F&SF in the early sixties.

He uses a particular sort of a distraction technique where he has a frontline plot going on with a lot of bells and whistles and flourishes, and at the same time is running a secondary or subplot in which he's scattering clues throughout. He distracts you with the foreground from the back-story enough so that when it all comes together at the end and the back-story suddenly pops up to the forefront and is a surprise ending, you are surprised even though he has laid the clues out fairly in front of you in the understory or the secondary line story. He's distracted you enough from them with the bells and whistles of the foreground story that when the two storylines mesh and the secondary storyline provides the surprise you actually are surprised.

I did a variant of this in this story. At least so I thought I was doing. Whether that came across or not, I don't know.

Spontaneous combustion is a Fortean phenomenon. You've always had a particular weakness for Fortean phenomenon, I believe.

Gardner Dozois: Yes, I've always been fond of Fortean phenomenon. In fact in London a couple of years before I wrote this story, I'd gotten an idea for a story about a plague of spontaneous combustion in the modern world. I never actually wrote that story, but some of the thinking and feeling I did about it no doubt went into the melt for this particular one.

There's a particularly grotesque image in there, of a burial pit in the Vienna catacombs with the stacked bones of hundreds of thousands of humans. Is that someplace you saw when you were in Europe?

Gardner Dozois: There actually is such a cathedral with bones of plague victims stacked underneath it in Vienna. I have been there and gone on the tour and looked through the hole in the wall and seen all the bones of the millions of Black Death victims stacked up there in heaps. For anybody who doubts the effectivity of biological weapons, I urge them to go and look at this. Perhaps they will change their minds.

This has always been a story that's a particular favorite of mine. It was not a story that was tremendously well received. Perhaps what I'm trying to do in this story did not come through as successfully as I wanted it to come through.

I think it's all of a piece, though, with the plague hooking up at a very deep level to people's basic meanness.

Gardner Dozois: I was trying to suggest that even though there is an objective cause, or an objective cause is suggested or given as a possibility, i.e., disease escaping from the biological warfare establishment, that it also matches up with what is happening in people's hearts and the spaces between people. Either in a direct metaphysical sense, or in the sense that if things were working well between people we wouldn't have the need for these kinds of establishments in the first place. There is a lot of that sort of symmetry going on in the story.

One sidelight on this is that I've been accused on a couple of occasions with this particular story of imitating Stephen King. Which is funny because when I wrote this story I had never even heard of Stephen King, let alone read anything by him. And no, I don't particularly think that Stephen King is imitating me either. I think this is just one way to write a contemporary horror story set in a rural background. It's one way that several authors have independently devised on their own. It probably owes a good deal to such writers as Fritz Leiber and others. In my case it owes a lot to Edgar Pangborn, who was my template in how to write rural stories. There's probably a jigger of Philip K. Dick thrown in here as well.

It does irk me occasionally though when someone says I'm trying to write a rip-off Stephen King story, just because it's set in rural New England and has a horrific element.

Of course you were born in Salem. In a way, your credentials are even better than his.

Gardner Dozois: This is just something that people have to put up with since Steve has become so famous. But no, for the record, I wasn't imitating Stephen King.

I do something here again, which is that I try to slip information across almost subliminally. I think on occasion I have taken this too far, to the point where nobody understands what I'm talking about in the story. I don't think it's quite that bad here. But there's one of the conversations you overhear in the background, people are talking about what is obviously a release of biological material from the factory. It slips by in the background. I had meant it to be something that would stick in your subconscious, and that you connect up consciously later when you get to the end of the story. But it may pass by so quickly that nobody notices it in the first place.

I suppose it depends on how much you expect out of your readers, whether you expect them to work hard enough to notice these clues or whether you expect them to just slide by on the surface. There are a few stories where if they just slide by on the surface, they are going to probably miss something.

I also mention, although I don't do much with it, I do throw in here that they are fighting a Vietnam-like war in South America. Which is one of the earlier mentions of this idea in science fiction, I believe. Tiptree may have beaten me to it. But certainly it was one of the earliest mentions of that particular idea, which has gotten a lot of play in the last ten years or so.

Another very minor prediction is that when he has the encounter with the car full of gypsy kids—which is an encounter that I actually had when I was in Skowhegan—in my own reality when it happened to me it was the usual pseudo-hippie longhair rednecks of the day, but in thinking of how I could make this more science-fictional for this story set slightly in the future I made the not terribly startlingly daring prediction that they would instead be skinheads, rather than having long hippie-like hair. This is hardly a terribly daring prediction, but it was something you didn't see much of in reality at the time. So, another minor interesting point.

There's a very careful pacing to the story, and I can't help feeling that much of the physical action, the dinner party for example with its downward psychological progression, has a symbolic, even a sacramental meaning as well as the literal one. Is that so?

Gardner Dozois: Yeah, there's a lot of symbolic stuff here. Practically everything he does has some symbolic significance. It would be tedious to work through it all and detail it.

"Joseph Farber met Liraun JeGenawen for the first time during the ceremony of the Alantene, the Mode of the Winter Solstice, the Opening-of-the-Gates-of-Dun, that was observed annually in the ancient city of Aie, on the North Shore of Shasine, on the world of Lisle. 'Lisle' was the Terran name, of course, after Senator Lisle Harris, the first human to visit the planet, and had come into common usage among the expatriate Terran population because the Earthmen professed great difficulty in pronouncing the native Weinunnach, 'Fertile Home.'"

"Strangers" was published in 1974 in Robert Silverberg's *New Dimensions IV*. The protagonist's name, Joseph Farber, suggests a number of things—Joseph, the human father of Christ, to begin with. Then Farber suggests faber or 'maker,' and in German literally means 'dyer,' which would be somebody who changes color or even somebody

**who dies. How much of this little knot of meaning is my
contribution and how much is yours?**

Gardner Dozois: I should probably just keep my mouth shut
and revel in the interpretations. But in fact, like most intellectual critics, you're giving me far too much credit for cleverness
that I don't actually possess. Michael Bishop did a big thing at
one point on the symbology of the name Farber. I believe
Michael Bishop said it was a homage to Philip José Farmer, but
that wasn't really true either. I think he had found some language in which he claimed that farber meant farmer, but none
of this was consciously intended. I'm afraid it's a much more
lowbrow reason. I just picked the name because it sounded like
a good name. I wanted a vaguely Germanic sounding name,
and that's what I picked. In fact—and you're *really* not going
to like this—I *actually* got the name by glancing at a pencil that
was on my desk next to the typewriter, when I was sitting there
staring through space and trying to come up with a name. On
the side of the pencil, it said "FARBER," and it struck me that
that was as good a name as any, so I used it. As you can see, I
worked out all the name symbolism here with exacting
intellectual rigor.

**To play the name game just one more time, I couldn't help
noticing the name for the planet, Weinnenach, supposedly
meaning 'Fertile Home.' Anybody who knows any German
whatsoever is going to have trouble hearing this as anything
but 'night of tears,' or possibly 'to bring to tears.' That must
have been lurking in the back of your head, that weinen
means 'to weep.'**

Gardner Dozois: Perhaps it was lurking in the back of my
head, but if so it never communicated with the front of my
head. I know I must be a terrible disappointment to deconstructionist critics, but again, as with all of the names in the

book, I just did it on the fly because it *sounded* good to me. If you want to read subconscious influences into it, that's certainly possible, but as far as *conscious* artistic control is concerned, all of the names I picked because they sounded euphonious to the ear when spoken aloud. There's no conscious symbolism or system at all to the names of things in this book. You can no doubt pick one out, as many clever critics can, but you're more or less putting in all that input yourself.

The background seems very densely worked out. The politics and the biology and the sociology and history of the planet and a lot of geography—there's an amazing amount of world-building in this, to a degree that you're not usually interested in doing in other stories, and I was wondering why?

Gardner Dozois: I haven't handled the alien worlds type of story very often in my career, and perhaps because this is one of the few times that I *have* handled alien worlds, I worked a lot of stuff in that I had been saving up and not using in other pieces of fiction. You have to understand that this story started out as a novelette that I was going to write for *New Dimensions* and it got longer and longer as I went along, working in the background. It's not so much that *Strangers* the novel is an expanded or padded version of the novella, as that the novella in the *first* place is a crunched or seriously compressed version of the novel. I found that in order to get the story into some sort of length that I could possibly sell to an anthology like *New Dimensions*, I had to seriously compress the plotline and more or less just summarize parts of the plot. "And then this happened and then that happened," and skip over a couple of months of real-time narrative in a paragraph or two. I did that to make a feasible novella out of it, as far as length is concerned. Then when I started thinking about making it into a novel, Don Keller and other critics had pointed out that these compressed sections were indeed compressed and could stand some expansion, and so I simply went back and unspronged the compressed sections and let them expand out to natural narrative length, or at least followed the action in those sections in real-time narrative somewhat more thoroughly than I had been able to in the novella version. So as I say, it's not so much that I expanded the novel as that I had taken a novel and crunched it down and compressed it into being a novella in the first place. Maybe that's got something to do with the density. I know a lot of my interest in the story was with playing with the background of the planet and making it as evocative and colorful as I could. I tried to work a lot of touches in it. I tried to work the same sort of evocativeness into the rituals and the religion and so forth that is part of the social background of the book.

The alien culture seems very mysterious at the beginning, but by the end when everything is explained, they turn out not to be mysterious at all. They're very nice people in fact, who simply don't want to discuss the intimate details of their culture. They're actually pretty generous, considering the damage this guy is doing.

Gardner Dozois: It's a variant of the hide-in-plain-sight technique, in that if Farber could ever *get* a straight explanation that he could understand, he probably *could* understand it. But he's never told anything in a straightforward enough fashion for him to understand before it's too late. In fact, the major philosophic point of the novel to me—this is true of the novella as well—is that neither he nor she ever understand *anything* that they say to each other in the entire course of the book. She's saying one thing and thinking that he's understanding and picking up the implication *behind* what she's saying. He's not understanding it. She's not understanding his lack of comprehension. He's saying things to her that *she's* not understanding. And so they both act on their misunderstanding, and this is one of the ironic implications of the title, of course. In spite of the fact that they're lovers and then husband and wife, they don't understand each other at all, they don't understand what they're *saying* to each other, and of course, by a not terribly difficult stretch this metaphor can be extended to the lives of ordinary human beings like us. Indeed I think that much of the time people *don't* understand what they're saying to each other in human cultures either, particularly where love and sex and male-female relationships are concerned. If there was ever any real communication between them, this tragedy could have been avoided. But indeed there is not. There are several key places in the plotline where one character thinks that he's saying one thing to the other and actually is conveying a quite different piece of information to the person listening. They misunderstand each other at practically every point.

This is partially because the aliens are very reticent about talking about this sort of thing. Everything they do say about the personal side of their lives is shrouded in webs of allegory and mythological reference and symbolism that she, perhaps unfairly, expects that he is going to understand.

On *his* side, he is also a somewhat blinkered protagonist himself in that he's not really all that intelligent, he's not really all that sensitive. He *ought* to pick up on a lot more than he does, but he doesn't pick up on it. So both of those things which keep them from really communicating are contributory to the central tragedy. Which is something they could have avoided if they were really understanding one another, but of course that's the point of the book, that they were not really understanding one another.

The title came from Leonard Cohen?

Gardner Dozois: Well, it *spiritually* comes from Leonard Cohen, but not exactly. There's a Leonard Cohen song that I like called "The Stranger Song," which is a very bleak song about male-female relationships. I thought of calling it "The Stranger" to make it more like the Leonard Cohen title, but then I realized that that really didn't convey the essence of the book—because, after all, it's not just *his* fault. There are *two* of them and they're both not understanding the other, so it would have to be "Strangers." So that's what I finally settled on. But the original impetus that started me thinking in that direction for a title came from the Leonard Cohen song.

In the beginning there's a little allegory about how in the wintertime the *opein* come out of the ocean, and possess men and drive them to evil deeds. This is obviously supposed to resonate with Farber. I was wondering if this is also a hint that the planet is undergoing a cultural winter, that eventually spring will come. Weren't there hints in the novel version that he'd screwed up, but the children might yet improve things?

Gardner Dozois: It's another one of my downbeat endings that you can rationalize as actually having a sort of a bleak optimism. He's fucked up hideously, he's caused his wife to die, it's a pretty black ending on the whole, except for the fact that although it's clearly not going to be easy, and it's clearly not going to be pleasant, he does seem set at the end of the novel on *raising* his children, and assumably making some sort of life for him and themselves. I mean, he's not committing suicide or throwing the babies into the garbage. There's a clear sense that he is going to take responsibility for the situation, and although in some ways it's not adequate recompense and he'll probably have to pay many years of dues for it, it's clear he is going to try to take care of the children. So in that sort of very restricted and weasely way, I suppose it's an upbeat or optimistic ending.

Along these lines it's interesting that I had sent this book to an English publisher for reprint last year and the editor told me the book was not downbeat enough for the eighties! I don't know what I could have done to make the book more downbeat. I guess if he had killed himself, or chopped all of his babies up with an axe, then maybe it would've been downbeat enough for the eighties.

What was the first part of your question, again?

Uh, about the *opein* driving men to evil deeds.

Gardner Dozois: Of course this would be the aliens' explanation of what had happened here. In fact toward the end there's someone out in the street outside his house wailing that he's been possessed by an *opein*. That would be at least the explanation of some of the aliens as to why he was acting in this strange way.

This is a very difficult story to reread, knowing that there is no hope.

Gardner Dozois: Well, maybe a smidgen of hope. Depending on how you define hope. It certainly doesn't end with an easy, Hollywood, they-lived-happily-ever-after type of hope. If you went back ten years down the line, although I'm sure he would have had a lot of difficulty and problems and tsurris, he might not say that he regretted that he was alive. So in that way it sort of has a sort of vague hope, I guess.

What happens, though, is very cruel, not only to her but to him. I was very strongly struck by the fact that the protagonist is doing the best he can. He really is trying all the way through, and the reason he fails is that he's inadequate. He's not a Heinlein individual, he's not a Campbellian superman. If he were a better person, perhaps he could make a go of it.

Being Gardner Dozois

Gardner Dozois: Indeed, that was quite intentional. He is a well-intentioned individual. He does do the best that he can. He does try hard. He just isn't perceptive or sensitive or smart enough to figure out what he ought to do. So he, helped by the aliens and by his wife in her own misunderstanding, makes a terrible hash of everything.

There was a sort of a vague polemical point in the back of my mind here, to show that a significant impact can be made upon a society by someone even if they are not particularly competent and Heinleinian and Campbellian. A non-superman. I suppose you could contrast this with my first story, "The Empty Man," where the character is a Campbellian superhero.

In "The Empty Man," one Earthman goes into the alien society and overthrows it all singlehandedly. Which, in fact, was a fairly common motif in the science fiction of the day. I think it may have been in the back of my mind to show that this one Earthman comes along and is not terribly effectual as far as overthrowing or changing a society. Now, if this novella had been written fifteen years before, it would've been pretty much expected that the Earthman *would* find out about this system and end up overthrowing it or changing it by the end of the story. But in fact he doesn't do that, and he's not effectual in overthrowing the society. At the same time he does have an odd effect on the society in spite of his ineffectuality, so those were some points I was sort of playing with. But they're not really vital for understanding the novella.

At one point Farber degenerates and you track his grim descent down through alcoholism and into the abyss. This is something you've done before, in "The Last Day of July," for example, showing somebody step by step stripped away from all social supports. It happens again in "The Storm," which we'll get to soon. I was wondering why you find this such a fascinating topic.

Gardner Dozois: I think I have a tendency myself to disintegrate similarly if I let myself do so. I learned years ago that I must take steps to prevent myself from sinking into this sort of morass. Many of the feelings that I show the protagonist having in "The Last Day of July" are feelings that I myself had in a less exaggerated fashion when I was living isolatedly in a house out in the woods in Milford, Pennsylvania. So it's something I know first-hand.

I should probably save this for "The Storm" section. But, again, the feelings that he goes through there are similar although more exaggerated to feelings that I myself experienced while living more or less on my own in a rundown apartment in the East Village. So I guess I have a tendency myself to sink into these sort of morasses, which tendency I have learned how to guard against for the most part over the years. Also, I've watched many other people break down under these sort of circumstances. And, of course, my own father was a borderline alcoholic for most of his life. Although he didn't really become incapable of functioning in society until a few years ago, when he became a totally burnt-out case. So I'm familiar with people sinking into sloughs of despond and madness, and it's perhaps not surprising that I write about this from time to time.

In many ways this is a very harrowing story. It really covers the ground. By the time you finish the story, you know you've read it.

Gardner Dozois: I guess it is a kind of a bleak story, on the whole. As I say, the basic message of the text is that people don't understand anything that they say to one another. Particularly men and women. There is a sort of an implicit optimism there in that I sort of imply that maybe if they were a little smarter and listened to each other a little more carefully, they *could* understand what they were saying to each other, but that probably doesn't make reading the novel any more jolly an experience.

You said something once that absolutely flabbergasted me. You said that you'd made up all the biology in there. The riff about forced fast evolution having its effect on the female reproductive tract, the change in stance making childbirth more difficult. This all reads very authoritatively as a change on human evolutionary history. Did you really make all this up, or am I misremembering that?

Gardner Dozois: Well, I made it up, but I didn't make it up out of whole cloth. I've read a fair amount of natural history in my day, after all. I don't remember exactly where I got this from. It was a rationalization for the system that I wanted to have set up for social reasons. But I do think that it's a rationalization that makes as much sense as the biological setups in most science fiction novels have to. It's scientifically rigorous enough to function as background rationalization in a science fiction novel. Which is about all you can really ask of such material. I think that the evolutionary tropes in the book are all *possible*, although some of them are less likely than others. But then again, some of the evolutionary arrangements that actually *do* exist are not terribly likely, either.

I remember you sitting in Washington Park...

Gardner Dozois: Yes! That's where I wrote most of it, on one of the table-and-bench sets in Washington Square Park in Philadelphia. I might add that the novel has had some interesting reactions. Several people liked it quite a bit. Other people didn't like it at *all*. I'm pretty sure that we tried to get a blurb out of Joanna Russ, and she contributed a blurb something along the order of "A novel so bad that it makes you want to hide under the sofa and howl!"

 Many people read the message of the novel as "biology is destiny," while actually the message is exactly opposite to that—they have the technology to fix or alleviate this situation;

they just don't *want* to. The problem is not in the biology, but in the *social* hardwiring...just as many women in Africa continue to clamor for their right to have hideously disfiguring clitorectomies, because that's the way things are *supposed* to be, it's the traditional way to do things. In this specific respect, as in several others, the book was a deliberate attempt to write a feminist novel. The feminists hated it, of course.

Other people reacted very negatively to what they interpreted as a hint of bestiality in his relationship with the alien woman, because she had six nipples. This pushed a lot of people's buttons, and they reacted very badly to the fact that woman was described as, not having fur exactly, but being sort of downy and having six nipples. This was more than some people could take.

One writer, who I probably shouldn't name, said that it was incredible to him that anybody could want to have sex with a creature who had six nipples and fur. To which my response was, "But people on Earth *today* have sex with cows and dogs, gerbils, cats, sheep..." So it doesn't seem like it's really that far a stretch of the imagination that they'd want to have sex with an alien woman who looked aesthetically pleasing to them in a plastic-form sense, even if she *did* have six nipples. But different strokes for different folks, I guess. That's why they make chocolate and vanilla.

I am somewhat disappointed that this novel's been out of print for more than ten years now, and I don't seem to be able to get it back into print. Which I find personally disappointing, since novels that came out at the same time that it did, and which I personally consider to be inferior, have gotten back into print two or three times in the interval. But that's the way the cookie crumbles.

It was David Hartwell, wasn't it, who got you to expand the novella into a novel?

Gardner Dozois: Yes, that's correct. When he was working at Berkley/Putnam.

He gave you a very short deadline on that, didn't he?

Gardner Dozois: You know, I don't remember exactly what the deadline was on that, but it *was* pretty short. I worked pretty intensively on it for about a month, I guess it was, to get the novella into shape as a novel.

I still have vivid memories of dropping by to visit Susan, and we'd chat for a while and then she'd look at her watch and say, "Well, time to pick up Gardner." We'd go off to the park, and you'd be hunched over a little table in the twilight, scribbling away. We'd lift you up. We'd lead you to a diner, have supper, and then afterwards you'd say, "Well, I'm off to write," and go looking for another diner where you could buy some coffee and spend the evening writing. Sort of the antithesis of the glamorous writer's life.

Gardner Dozois: Part of the reason for this was that, at least in the summer, my Quince Street apartment became practically uninhabitable because of the heat. It was much too hot to do any work at the typewriter. So I would find a stoop or a stone stair somewhere in the neighborhood, or the park and the table-and-benches, and I would sit there and write in my notebook tablet. This sounds romantic, but it wasn't so much a matter of romance as a matter of necessity. It was just too hot to work in the apartment.

And frankly with an apartment of that size—and it was a very small apartment—with another person, Susan, and a very active child, Christopher, jammed into it, it often was too distracting to work there, even if the temperature was all right. So this is the genesis of my slouching melancholily around the neighborhood with a notebook, like some consumptive nineteenth-century Romantic poet, and sitting on people's doorsteps and scribbling fragments of one thing and another.

You did the last few days' writing in New York, in somebody's apartment?

Gardner Dozois: I was staying at Trina King's apartment, crashing there while I was consulting David about the novel, and I actually wrote one of the chapters in my notebook while sitting on the floor in the bathroom. Next to the toilet, appropriately enough, for all you hostile critics out there. From time to time, someone would come in to go to the bathroom, and I would nod politely at them. I had to work in the bathroom because there was someone sleeping in the living room, so that had to be dark, and the bedroom had to be dark because Trina was sleeping in there. So the only place I could work was in the bathroom, where the light could be on. This is the kind of thing that makes me smile when young writers tell me they can't work without an office of their own and a word-processor. Yeah, I finished a chapter in the bathroom there.

Do you remember which chapter?

Gardner Dozois: Actually I do, although I probably shouldn't admit this. It was the chapter where the woman who's been caught taking contraceptive drugs is being chased by the mob who want to kill her. The woman protagonist interferes and saves her from the mob. That was the chapter that I was writing in the bathroom.

There, I've given someone a real hook to slice me up with there!

"The sky had been ominous all that afternoon—a lurid yellow-green to the south, darkening overhead to blood and rust and soot. East, out over the ocean, there were occasional bright flashes and flares in rapid sequence, all without sound, as though a pitched artillery battle were being fought somewhere miles away and out of earshot."

"The Storm" first appeared in 1975 in *Future Corruption*. Wasn't that one of Roger Elwood's anthologies?

Gardner Dozois: Yes, it was. Which probably shows that it wasn't a story at the top of my form, since I couldn't manage to do anything better with it than sell it to an Elwood anthology. I forget how I ended up selling that story to Elwood, but he was unavoidable if you were working in science fiction in the early seventies. He was just all over the place. He was like Chun the Unavoidable. No matter what alley you ran down, there he would be at the end of it. King of the Salvage Markets. He got all the trunk stories writers couldn't sell to anyone else, like this one.

The story begins with Paulie watching the storm come in, the lightning like a pitched artillery battle, shivering with the premonition of something big coming in. It's a rather Bradburyesque section. Which would make the whole story something like Bradbury gone bad, I suppose.

Gardner Dozois: Sour Bradbury. Spoiled Bradbury that's been left out of the refrigerator too long. Bradbury with fungus on it.

I always wondered what happened to the kids in Bradbury's stories after they grow up. But I guess now we know.

Gardner Dozois: I was deliberately writing somewhat purple there. I was writing at the top of my evocative ability at the moment. And it *is* somewhat overwritten, but it still has a nice touch here and there. My entire career has been an attempt to find ways to be evocative *without* being purple, to be verbally lush without overwriting. It's a balance that can easily tip one way or the other.

There's a passage in which the coming storm has drawn all the birds away. "Later," you write, "in another county, it would rain birds." Which is a nice poetic touch, but also sounds a lot like Charles Fort.

Gardner Dozois: It's probably a better sentence and image than the story deserves, actually. But yeah, I have read a lot of Charles Fort, which is probably another conversational line we could get into at some time.

Actually, I like the story. I think it's a good story.

Gardner Dozois: Well, it's not my *worst* by any means. Although I think that I tried to convey more information by implication than was really practical. I probably should have conveyed some of the information behind the story in a more straightforward manner; it's almost information conveyal by sublimation in a couple of places. It probably is not fair to the reader to expect them to ferret all this out. It probably would have been a more successful story if I'd brought it up closer to the surface.

When Paulie is out in the storm, he finds a feather on the

sidewalk. Then he finds another feather, and another. With mounting excitement he follows this trail of feathers, gathering them up until he has a whole handful. Then at the end of this trail he finds a dead bird. He stops and the feathers fall and swirl about his feet. Several things struck me about this. First of all, it's very cinematic, obviously. Secondly it's almost an absurdist joke—of *course* what you'd find at the end of the trail is a dead bird. But more significantly, you're also giving the plot away: what happens to Paul later is a process of one by one losing his feathers, as it were.

Gardner Dozois: That actually was in the back of my mind when I wrote it. I did myself, when young—which I think is the opening line of a poem—I did myself, when young come across a trail of feathers in a similar fashion and follow it and find a dead bird. And I felt the same emotions that he does in the story. I think that even at the time, I was to some degree aware of the symbolic or mythic import of all this. It gave me a chill, anyway.

This in a way is a very black story. In a way, it's blacker than "Strangers," in that basically it shows a man becoming tired of himself, disillusioned with his life, and working with a large burden of guilt and shame and self-revulsion and self-loathing. What he actually does is to destroy himself. The New York City passages, where he is an adult, show him becoming increasingly more dissatisfied with himself and his life, and show his self-loathing becoming greater and greater, until he dives into his own past and destroys himself as a boy.

So, in a way, that's the dead bird at the end of the trail of feathers, and he even follows the trail backwards to find his younger self, in a metaphorical sense. So you're right, that is one of the central metaphors here.

The basic genesis of the story came from a semi-dream that I had, where I got the idea that you could *judge* yourself, that there was some capacity of the mind that would enable you to judge yourself and destroy yourself retroactively, if you had enough self-hatred to do so. Having once hit on that, I eventually came to the idea that the *rest* of the story had to be written from the viewpoint of his younger self, when magic and enchantment were still a possibility for him.

At one point, I had toyed with the idea of mingling this line as a counterpoint line with the story in the "The Last Day of July," since they're almost symmetrically opposed. In "The Storm," the character grows more and disillusioned with himself, fades away from the world, fades deeper and deeper into his own reality, the world receding more and more into the background. Until he reaches the decision that he can't exist in the world anymore, so he'll destroy himself, and he does destroy himself retroactively by destroying the child that he was. In "The Last Day of July," the character goes through a similar process, where he fades away from the world and fades back and back. But he, rather than destroying himself retroactively in the past, disappears from the world altogether, and takes up an existence in some other area of creation, some other world, with at least the implication that this is a hopeful thing, that he will get along better there than he did in our world. I was going to mingle these two storylines in a complex counterpoint structure, switching from one to the other. But the structure was *too* complex, and I could see, without actually doing it, that it wasn't going to fly. It wasn't going to work. So instead I used as a counterpoint line the scenes that are narrated from the viewpoint of his younger self. Which probably does work better, anyway, in terms of this particular story.

So then "The Last Day of July" and "The Storm" were written about the same time?

Gardner Dozois: I think that I actually wrote "The Last Day of July" first. I think that I had in my notebook a series of notes for a story that is roughly synonymous with the New York passages in "The Storm," and that I had thought about working these in as a counterpoint line at the time I was writing "The Last Day of July." But I didn't, and later I worked them up into the New York section of "The Storm."

As I say, most of the things that are described in the New York line of this story actually *did* happen to me. I even felt similar to the way the character feels, although in nowhere near as exaggerated a fashion. For me it was a passing mood. For him it's a central obsession. So I did exaggerate the way that he felt. But feelings at least similar in kind did flit through me while I was living in that apartment.

The apartment as described is the apartment that I lived in in New York at the time. Which also features in my story, "Machines of Loving Grace."

The "apartment on East Tenth Street between First and Avenue A," the "seedy fifth floor walk-up" with more cockroaches than I ever want to see in my life?

Gardner Dozois: That's it. Almost everything in the New York line did happen to me. The realtor really did come in without any notice and rip a gigantic hole in my bathroom wall, leaving the apartment exposed to the open air, with birds flying in and out, and then go off and leave and not come back to fix this for several weeks. So that all did happen.

In fact, one of the central metaphors of the story that finally drives him to conclude that his life is no good and he should go back and destroy himself, i.e. the scene where he sits down at his typewriter to type and cockroaches come boiling out of the typewriter mechanism, also happened to me. Although my reaction to that, perhaps fortunately, perhaps not, was not as extreme as the reaction of the character in the story.

I should probably add that many of the observations in the young Paulie section are also things that I observed myself when young. We had several big hurricanes come through, for instance, and I observed those. And of course the dead bird incident and several others were part of my youthful experience.

You have throughout, I hate to say thematic, but consistent references to Godelized messages, lights seen in the storm flashing like semaphored messages to God, unreadable messages everywhere. When Paul is degenerating, the language his landlord speaks becomes barely human and almost unrecognizable. There seems to be a sort of baffled semiotics at work here.

Gardner Dozois: You can probably tell that I am not terribly perceptive myself, in that many of my characters stumble around through the stories being baffled by all of the information that they're not understanding, that people and cosmic forces are trying to convey to them. This probably goes back to an intuition that I mentioned when discussing "A Dream at Noonday," an intuition that I have on a mystical level and have had for some time, that we are constantly surrounded by omens, if you will, or information, or *connections* that we don't perceive. That we're surrounded by a huge network of unseen connections that, if we could only *recognize* them, would lead us to understand that all parts of our life and the cosmos were connected in odd ways to other parts.

Unfortunately, I mostly *don't* perceive these connections. So that may be where the baffled, blinkered lack of comprehension that these characters display towards the cosmos comes from.

On the other hand, if young Paulie *were* able to perceive the semaphore messages to God that are flickering all about him, he might not necessarily like what they have to say. Since the gods are not particularly interested in whether we like what they're talking about or not.

In a weird way this is sort of a crossroads story for you.

There are lots of other stories that pass through. In addition to "Last Day in July," there's a scene where Paul sits motionless on the couch and over a long period of time the sunlight moves across the room, but he does not move. Which is very much like the opening pages of "Executive Clemency." When Paulie discovers that something has happened, his future self has wreaked vengeance on him, he looks around and realizes that the air, the house, his mother—they were not the same ones he'd had before. Which is very much like "Playing the Game."

Gardner Dozois: Probably like "Chains of the Sea," too. But yeah, you're right, it has some points of similarity to "Playing the Game." It's interesting that you mention the sunlight moving across the room, because although I hadn't thought of it before, that is indeed a bit like the opening of "Executive Clemency." The funny thing there is that the opening of "Executive Clemency," with the sunlight moving across the floor, was actually written by Jay Haldeman. And the *really* funny thing about that is that he claims in his essay for the collaborative short story collection that he had written it that way as a parody of my own writing!

So this knot is particularly convoluted.

I like the story, probably better than you do. But I think it has one weakness, which is that the casual reader is probably not going to realize the extent of the storm. Anybody is going to catch on that it's a big storm, since it's knocking over houses and flattening trees and such. But there's a one-word clue when the radio says "...Roche..." rather like Citizen Kane saying "Rosebud," which gives the whole game away. You're talking about the Moon coming within the Roche limit and smashing into the Earth and destroying not only humanity but all life as well. How did you come to choose such an extreme way of killing off your protagonist?

Gardner Dozois: You're quite right; as I said earlier, I think that I made a mistake technically in this story, in that I expected too much of the reader. I *did* give him a clue, but to expect him to figure all this out from the clue that is given is perhaps too much to expect of a casual reader. I probably should have brought this up closer to the surface, so that it would be more easily graspable. If I had, the story might have had more impact.

Yes, this is indeed the Moon falling below the Roche limit and the Earth being destroyed as a result. I probably could have had him go back and destroy himself in some more mundane manner that would only affect *him*. And indeed that would probably have been karmically more wholesome. But he sort of turns away from life in disgust and in doing so picks an alternative to manifest that involves wiping life itself off of the Earth. Which, of course, is not very fair to the *rest* of the people, but indicative of the mental state that he's in.

I think the real reason why I picked this, rather than some other way of having him retroactively kill himself, is that it ties in with a rather odd childhood experience of mine. When I was a little kid—oh, I guess I was about four, maybe five, somewhere in that vicinity—we had a big hurricane come through Massachusetts. And my mother, who is a very imaginative woman but never received any formal education, and as a result was always prone to get things wildly wrong, somehow misinterpreted something that she heard on television or on the radio to understand that the moon had fallen down out of its orbit and was going to destroy the Earth. And her reaction to this—which remember was in the middle of a hurricane, which even at the time never really made any sense to me—was to bundle me up and rush out into the storm, and rush down to the seaside. We stood there at the seaside, watching enormous waves crash into the rocky foreshore. And she was hysterical, and, of course, I had just been told by my mother that the world was coming to an end, and so *I* believed it.

The emotional loading behind that probably explains adequately enough why I chose this unlikely and rococo scenario to bring about the end of the world in this particular story.

At the end, Paulie hears his future self crying in his head and regretting it. So the punishment is absolute—not only is he absolutely punished, but he's sorry that he's absolutely punished. It just occurred to me that this chimes with "Solace," your most recent published story. Do you have any theories why this one story would have so many ties back and forth to stories throughout your *oeuvre*?

Gardner Dozois: Gee, I didn't even know that I had an *oeuvre*. I thought I'd had those taken out. But, no, I'm not really sure why. Some of it was planned. Some of it, like the Moon falling down, rushed in because of psychological reasons in the back of my head somewhere.

I hadn't thought of the similarity to "Solace" before, but you're quite right, there is a similarity there. I'm really not sure why. Perhaps I tend to think that we *are* our own judges, and ultimately responsible for punishing or destroying ourselves if we think that we deserve it. Other than that, I really couldn't say.

I haven't thought of this as a really successful story. Perhaps it's not successful because too many parts of other stories are churning around in it. It probably would have been a more successful story, for instance, if I had picked some way of him doing himself in that was less unlikely and rococo, and more reasonable. So I don't know. There are good parts to this story, but on the whole I'm not sure if it's entirely successful. Certainly it's never been reacted to very enthusiastically by any of the audience.

One little technical detail which you may find amusing—as you probably know, I'm very concerned with finding the exactly right last line for a story. I think last lines of stories are very important, and a bad last line for a story can diminish the value of even a good story by, say, forty percent. So I spend a lot of time trying to come up with last lines of stories. I've been known to spend weeks trying to come up with the right last line of a story. And here, I thought of three possible last lines for the end of the story. I couldn't decide which one to use, so I used them all in sequence.

You may find this particularly amusing because exactly the same thing happened when we were writing "Afternoon at Schrafft's." Where again three last lines occurred to me and I couldn't decide which one to use, so I put all three of them in, in sequence.

"George Rowan's only chance of escape came to him like a benediction, sudden and unlooked-for, on the road between Newburyport and Boston."

The next story is "The Visible Man," which appeared in 1975 in the December issue of ANALOG edited by Ben Bova. It certainly is a departure to see you in ANALOG.

Gardner Dozois: I won the Analytical Laboratory poll for that month, too. Which is rather amazing. Campbell was probably spinning in his grave.

In a weird way this is an ANALOG puzzle-story. You have the resourceful protagonist in a very bad situation, and he's given one shot at freedom. Using only his wits and resources, how can he escape against enormous odds? Except that it reads rather like the day that the Enemy took over ANALOG: it turns out that it's no use being a

Campbellian individual because the government is corrupt, and the deck is stacked.

Gardner Dozois: To a certain extent this was deliberate and planned. I made the surface as much like an ANALOG puzzle adventure story as I could. But, of course, the surface is not really what's happening in the story. What's happening is underneath the surface, where the protagonist can't perceive it or get at it. The understory is quite different.

I'm sure Ben realized this, but he was tolerant enough to allow it to go through.

There's a reference on the first page to "the expected psychological torture." So again it's the Purloined Letter, you tell everyone what's happening, and then proceed to not let them know what you're doing.

Gardner Dozois: Well, yes, indeed, and that's what I did. And I thought I had played fair there by mentioning that in this society people *are* subjected to various psychological tortures that drive them insane again and again. So when it turns out that this is indeed one of them, it shouldn't come as too much of a surprise. Or, hopefully it *will* come as a surprise, but not one that will infuriate the reader as being unfair.

I also, come to think of it, just now realized that there's also a parallel to "Solace" in this story as well. The protagonist's job in "Solace" is to drive people insane by creating false psychological realities for them and manipulating them in such a fashion as to break down the will of the people that are being subjected to this psychological torture. So there's a thematic similarity to "Solace" there too.

One of the people running the protagonist refers to him as a political prisoner. Is this something you put in to make the protagonist more acceptable to the reader?

Gardner Dozois: He's clearly not an ordinary prisoner, someone who's knocked over a Seven-Eleven or mugged an old lady
for drug money. Don't forget this is also coming out of the
Sixties, since this story was written within spitting distance of
the end of the decade. So perhaps I worked some of that sort of
feeling into the story.
 There's a definite hint of persecution. He's not just a crim-
inal, somebody who deserves to be punished. He's someone
who has fallen afoul of the gears of the State, or the
Corporation, or whoever's running the show here, and is being
crushed for that particular reason. I didn't think it was really
important what he had done. That's almost beside the point.
Although I could have easily made up some crime for him to
have committed, I didn't particularly want to. I left it deliberately vague. Although there is a hint, as you say, that he's a
political prisoner and that his persecution is undeserved in any
karmic sense.

**His problem is that he's visible but cannot see any other
living animal or human. Which I guess is just a stronger
than usual metaphor for alienation?**

Gardner Dozois: I've always been big on alienation. Most of
my characters are alienated in one way or another. Most of
them are psychically hampered in one way or another too, or
not terribly bright. Which I suppose says something unsavory
about *me* psychologically. This is the way in which this particular character is hampered.
 The idea came to me originally...Well, it's two-pronged.
There's one which is a respectable intellectual source for the
idea, and one which is the stupid—or actual—source for the
idea. I had been reading about some very creepy hypnotic experiments in which a person could be hypnotized and made unable
to see some specific object, even though it was in the room with
him. You could hypnotize someone and make yourself invisible

to him, and even though you were in the room, they would not notice or respond to you. Or you could hypnotize somebody and make them unable to see, say, lamps or television sets. They would go about unable to perceive them thereafter. That made me wonder, of course, what kinds of things we might in our ordinary lives be unable to see that were all around us, things that Someone had given us orders *not* to see, even though they surrounded us and brushed by us every day.

More mundanely, and stupidly, which is probably closer to the actual impetus for stories, I was listening to the song, "I Only Have Eyes for You," at one point after this, and the line connected up with the stuff I was reading, and I thought that it would be interesting to have a situation where that was *literally* true.

It was also one of a series of bizarre ways to punish people, as far as correctional-type punishment, institutionalized punishment, is concerned, that I was thinking about at one time or another. Enforced aging—so that you'd literally "do time," they'd artificially age you the number of years in your sentence —was another.

So all this sort of came together.

At the end, the fox-faced man says that their ability to torture the protagonist makes them gods. And he is sort of buffeted by the gods in the story. I was wondering about your comments on that, since in those stories of yours where people *don't* assume the role of the gods, the universe is sort of aloofly neutral.

Gardner Dozois: I do tend to think of the universe as aloof, rather than actively hostile, for the most part. On the other hand, going back to what I said about my intuition that there are floods of coded information and connections going on around us all the time that we do not perceive, it's possible that your life actually *is* being directed by people like this, who are bustling unseen around you, making you do things you don't particularly want to do, and herding you down chutes of one sort or another, for their own reasons, to achieve their own goals.

Actually, I don't really believe this, because I don't think that anybody would *bother* to take the time to do this with me. It wouldn't be worth the trouble. So that keeps me a saving hair's-breadth away from clinical paranoia. Because although I do think that it's possible that this *could* be going on all around me, I don't think anybody would actually take the trouble to bother to *do* it. So that probably keeps me out of an institution.

It's also possible, by the way, that the fox-faced man and his friends are *themselves* being herded and manipulated by beings that *they're* not aware of—perhaps it's an infinite-regress cycle. "Big bugs have little bugs..."

You borrowed the title of this story for your first short story collection, *The Visible Man*. Did you just like the title, or is this a particularly favorite story?

Gardner Dozois: I like the story. It's not my favorite in the book. I picked the title—or rather, David and I together agreed on the title—mostly because it seemed to me to be the story title that made the best book title. None of the others seemed to work out that well. "Chains of the Sea" had been used as a book title already; that's what the three-novella volume that Silverberg edited was called. "A Special Kind of Morning" didn't seem to work. "Horse of Air," obviously, was right out. "The Storm" was not particularly snappy. So by a process of elimination we arrived at *The Visible Man*. Although I think "Flash Point" would've made just as good a title, perhaps a better one in some ways.

But nevertheless, we chose "The Visible Man." Where the title "The Visible Man" comes from is, of course, so obvious that I don't need to elucidate it. At least I *hope* I don't need to elucidate it.

―――――――――

"The four-seater Beechcraft Bonanza dropped from a gray sky to the cheerless winter runways of Fargo Airport. Tires touched pavement, screeched, and the single-engine plane taxied to a halt. It was seven o'clock in the morning, February 3, 1959."

―――――――――

After "The Visible Man," there's a hiatus before your next publication in the April, 1981 issue of PENTHOUSE. "Touring" was your first story after a long dry spell.

Gardner Dozois: Well, yeah, in fact I *had* gone through a long dry spell. "The Visible Man" was I think the last short story that I did before the dry spell set in.

It's a little less cut and dried than it seems, in that in the middle of the "dry spell" I did expand "Strangers" from a novella to the novel version. But there's no doubt that there's a period of two or three years in there during which I was not writing much. During that period I also did some sporadic work from time to time on my years-in-the-making, cast-of-thousands, probably never-to-be-published novel *Nottamun Town*. Which still sits in my files at home. So I did do some work from time to time during this period, but I never actually produced any finished stories. And I did anthologies and I did some editing work. But it was still a long dry spell for me, regardless.

It began breaking up sometime, I believe, in '79. Now, I wasn't keeping up my work calendar, so I don't have the exact dates. But I believe that we started work on "Touring" sometime in '79. I know that it was finished in time for me to read it to the audience at Armadillocon in October, 1980, when I was the guest of honor down there. My guess is that we started working on it in '79 or early in '80.

I do remember fairly clearly that it was the first short story that I had worked on in quite a while. Shortly thereafter I also began work on "Executive Clemency," another story from that period. So I had actually begun writing again somewhere around '79 or '80. Although I didn't begin in any significant volume until 1981, after I had nearly died and been hospitalized. Paradoxically, after I got back on the street after that, I felt a rush of creative energy and for the next three or four years produced, for me, a fair volume of work.

But the dry spell was beginning to break up by sometime in '79, when I began working with you guys on "Touring."

Maybe I shouldn't admit this. But as I remember it, what happened was that Jack Dann had come by to visit, and the three of us were hanging around your old Quince Street apartment, talking about art and planning anthologies and plotting out novels and such. I went home around three in the morning, and when I came back the next day, you guys had plotted out a story in its entirety which you thought I should help you write. So that as I recall it, I had no input into what the story was about. Where did you get the idea for this story?

Gardner Dozois: I recall that we had worked this all out the night before, but it's possible that you came over the next day. Basically, we wanted to get you to write the story with us because we were too lazy to duplicate the research that you had just gotten through doing on Buddy Holly and Janis Joplin. Although I did end up doing some of it anyway, as it turned out.

The story arose out of Jack and me sitting around talking. I'm pretty sure it was Jack who made some sort of joke or remark about at least Elvis and either Buddy Holly or Janis Joplin playing together. I'm not sure he had worked them all into the same sentence, although it's possible. And I immediately seized upon the story possibilities of this.

As I describe in my introduction to our collaborative short story collection, *Slow Dancing Through Time*, one of the reasons I started to come out of my dry period at this point was because I had been doing a lot of workshopping with you and with Jack, at first individually and then later on together. I had been workshopping portions of Jack's novel, *The Man Who Melted*, with him, giving him advice both on it as a novel and how he could pull chunks of it out as individual short stories. And during this same period or a little before, I had been workshopping some of your early stories with you, and I think all of this workshopping sort of loosened the ice and got my own creative juices going again. The workshopping also processed naturally into our writing short stories together. For me at least, it was an imperceptibly gradual process where at one point we were all workshopping stories together, and the next point down the line we were writing stories together. It just seemed like a natural transition.

As I said, I think the exact genesis of this story was a joke or remark about Elvis and Janis Joplin playing together that Jack made. The plot blossomed in my mind in an instant after he said that. I perceived of it immediately as a Twilight Zone episode, and that's indeed the way that I plotted it.

I remember you said at the time that when you were writing a Twilight Zone episode sort of story, the most important thing was that nobody in the story was to ever mention the words "Twilight Zone."

Gardner Dozois: Yes. Good point, good point.

You said it would give away the show.

Gardner Dozois: No, having Janis look around and say, "Hey,

this is just like a Twilight Zone episode!" probably would not have worked very well.

If you wish, you can imagine the ghost of Rod Serling looming up at the end of the story to provide closing commentary. But I do think of it as a Twilight Zone episode, and in fact I think it would have made a good one if they could have found people to adequately portray Buddy Holly and Janis Joplin and Elvis. George R. R. Martin turned it down when he was the story editor for the new TWILIGHT ZONE TV show, but I still think he was wrong.

Now I don't know how *you* remember this. It's my memory, or partial memory, that our original scheme for this story was that each one of us was going to take a character and write the scenes in which that character was involved. You were supposed to write Janis Joplin, I was going to do Buddy Holly, and Jack of course, who's a much bigger Elvis fan than either of us, was going to do Elvis. But as I recall, we soon found that this was a really unworkable plan technically, and abandoned it, and all of us ended up writing scenes using the other writers' characters.

As I remember it, the big sticking point was Jack, who it turned out only liked Elvis' music and in fact knew nothing at all about Elvis' private life. He just wasn't the fan type— it's hard to picture Jack running down to Graceland for a weekend.

Gardner Dozois: I think he did know *some* things about Elvis' background. I seem to recall that I had Elvis asking where the nearest bar was in an early draft of a scene and Jack pointing out that Elvis didn't drink and made a big point about it. So we worked that into the story instead.

It's hard to explain to people who weren't there, how these collaborations actually worked. Even though this is supposed to be an interview with me, your perspective on many of these stories is going to be just as germane, if not more so. Usually one person would do a partial draft, another person would do another rough draft to the end, and then another person would come through and do a unifying draft, tying everything together and smoothing out the rough edges.

That wasn't always the method that we used, but it's the method we used more often than not.

It usually ended up with you doing the final draft, because Jack and I both like your prose stick.

Gardner Dozois: I did tend to do the unifying draft, maybe because of my experience as a story doctor, which goes fairly far back, and maybe because you and Jack had already become inured to my inflicting my advice on such matters on you anyway, in the workshops. People often ask me how it's possible for three people to do a collaboration. Particularly three people whose writing styles and concerns are as different as yours and mine and Jack's. I do think that one of the keys to it is to have somebody do a final unifying draft to make sure everything is as homogeneous as possible. Also, if there are two different competing versions of the same theme, you need someone to decide which one should go into the manuscript and which one should not. So I do think you need somebody to do that, or at least it makes it easier if you have somebody to do that.

This is a departure for you in many ways, in that the characters are pick-ups from the culture, and the story is far less personal than, if not all your previous stories, than most of your previous stories, which come from various parts of your life, and this is more, uh, more like the way the rest of us write science fiction.

Gardner Dozois: The obvious factor is that I wasn't creating this story alone, but was creating it with two other writers. That alone should be sufficient to explain why its themes and colors and concerns are different from what they had been in my solo work. Would I on my own hook have written a story about either these three people together or any of these three people singly? I tend to doubt that I would have. But the fact that we came up with this story together and were working on it together, required me to write about these people and these themes, where on my own hook I would not have.

And I think that was a good thing in a way. Because it enabled me to get into some material that I probably wouldn't have gotten into on my own. Which is I think one of the strengths of collaboration.

"It looked like rain again, but Michael went for his walk anyway. The park was shiny and empty, nothing more than a cement square defined by four metal benches. Piles of rain-soaked garbage were slowly dissolving into the cement. Pterodactyls picked their way through the gutter, their legs lifting storklike as they daintily nipped at random pieces of refuse."

The next story is "A Change in the Weather," which is something of a sore point with me.

Gardner Dozois: Yes, you should perhaps discuss the origin of *this* one.

You and Jack wrote this one...

Gardner Dozois: Yeah. With a little help from our friend.

I've told my version in *Slow Dancing Through Time*. Maybe you should tell your version of it here.

Gardner Dozois: My version of this is pretty close to your version, actually. You and Jack and I were sitting around in my living room in my Quince Street apartment at one point, drinking more wine than we should have, and talking and larking around and discussing various projects. As I recall, I had a new typewriter and a new ribbon for the typewriter, and I wanted to test my typewriter ribbon. At one point or another in the evening one or the other of us would go over to the typewriter and type something out on it to test the ribbon. And Jack and I were discussing a story we were plotting (which story I might add parenthetically, we still have not written, like, six years later or more, however long it has been), about an old man who finds himself growing younger. Jack had wandered over to the typewriter and typed the opening sentence of this story, which involved an old man sitting on a park bench despondently, with the grey rain beating down on his head and soaking the piles of garbage around him and so forth. A very downbeat, moody sentence. Then Michael wandered over to the typewriter and wrote an additional paragraph of *parody* of this opening sentence, where the old man was surrounded by pterodactyls which were picking through the trash, picking out choice bits of garbage and popcorn and so forth. He had done this as a satire on Jack's opening sentence...

I wouldn't have made fun of it if Jack could have explained coherently what the story was about.

Gardner Dozois: So later on, after Michael went home, I went over and sat down myself behind the typewriter, and the incongruity of the image of the old man sitting there with the pterodactyls wandering around him, and he's totally ignoring them—obviously they're commonplace—struck an ironic nerve in me and I wrote the rest of the story, another page or two in which he slogs his way home through various other kinds of dinosaurs, and we have an appalling pun at the end to finish this up. The next day, when Michael came by, we showed him this manuscript, and since he had contributed part of the opening paragraph, we offered to cut him in on the deal and make it a three-way collaboration and put his name on it. But you, as I recall, were appalled by the shoddy commerciality of all this—

I was too High Art for that.

Gardner Dozois: —and told me that you in no way wanted your name on this little piece of tripe. And besides, we wouldn't be able to sell it for very much money anyway. And, of course, as these things work out, we sold the story on our first try to the highest-paying fiction market in America. It sold to PLAYBOY on the first attempt. To everyone's consternation, including myself and Jack's and my agent's, but I think Michael's more than anyone else.

Yes, well, I guess I showed you.

Gardner Dozois: Didn't you once figure out how much money you would've made if you'd left your name on it?

It was something like forty dollars or fifty dollars a word.

Gardner Dozois: I'm not sure there's really much else that needs to be said about that story. It certainly doesn't have any deep significance of any sort. Even a deconstructionist critic would find it hard to find much meat into which to sink his semiotic teeth in this particular little souffle. It is ironic, however, that it sold to PLAYBOY. Especially since it has no sexual element whatsoever.

"Nicky the Horse was a thin, weaselly-looking man with long dirty black hair that hung down either side of his face in greasy ropes, like inkmarks against the pallor of his skin."

"Disciples" appeared in the December, 1981, issue of PENTHOUSE, fiction editor Kathy Green. You were on a streak there, selling to the slicks all of a sudden.

Gardner Dozois: There were a few years there, in the beginning of the eighties, where various collaborators and I were selling a fair amount to the slicks. I also sold a fair number of stories to PENTHOUSE when Kathy Green was the fiction editor there, and one to PLAYBOY.

The interesting part about all of these stories, including the collaborative stories, was that they were not penetrating the genre market at the time. The digest-sized SF magazine market of the early eighties was pretty resistant to all of this stuff. It was too weird, too gonzo, too sacrilegious for them. It mentioned rock and roll, it made fun of Jesus, it had drugs in it. A lot of this stuff was just beyond the pale as far as the digest-sized SF world of the early eighties was concerned.

The interesting part about that was that what was being rejected from ASIMOV'S and F&SF and AMAZING was being picked up by big-money paying slicks like OMNI and PENTHOUSE and PLAYBOY. We didn't plan it that way. We didn't sit down and say, "Let's write these stories and penetrate and conquer the slick magazine market." We weren't that bright. It just sort of happened by accident. The SF magazines weren't buying them, so we sent them to the slick magazines, and the slick magazines *were* buying them. Which I find amusing.

A few years later, when the digest-sized SF magazine market had loosened up a little bit, we did sell reprints of several of them to various of the magazines. But the initial penetration was with the slick markets and not with the genre markets. We even sold one of them to a magazine, HIGH TIMES, where it appeared with a girlie-magazine-like gatefold of a marijuana plant.

Yes, I remember that. "Disciples" starts out with a street-Christian hustler out begging for spare change and getting freebies on the street. I think it's been long enough that you dare explain how this all began.

Gardner Dozois: Well, I hope so. One of the genesises of this certainly was that for several years at the end of the seventies and the beginning of the eighties, there was a group of evangelical Jesus freaks who were hustling around Center City. They referred to themselves as being from the Lamb House—Lord House was the version I used in the story—and they'd come up to you in the laundromat or something and they would say, "Come to the big Lamb-Out tonight, man. We're going to Lamb-Out with Jesus!" And various weird things of that sort. Then they would try to hustle money off of you. And, of course, this is one of the genesis-points of this story.

When I actually came to write the story, rather than the fresh-faced young Jesus freaks that you would actually see, I made the Jesus freak more like a burnt-out old street junkie. I'm not sure why it occurred to me to do that, but it seemed more interesting texturally to have the hustler be an old street hustler veteran rather than a young kid. It's sort of like this is his last resort. He's gone through all the infrastructure above that, and he's down to hustling for Jesus now. It's sort of like the last rationalization that he can come up with.

You have a very careful description of Center City in there. In fact I once took the story and using its directions was able to follow the protagonist's wanderings back and forth through Center City.

Gardner Dozois: The low-life junkie Jesus freak tour of Center City, Philadelphia! Well, of course, as was my usual wont, I wrote most of this story sitting on one person's stoop or another. So the fact that I was describing the area of Center City in which I was sitting at the time is probably not terribly surprising.

This was the first solo story that I had written since "The Visible Man." I had worked on the two collaborations, "Touring" and "Executive Clemency," sometime in the period 1979-80. But this, after I was released from the hospital, was my first *solo* story in quite a while. In fact I wrote it within a week of being released from the hospital. Phrases in the hustler's voice just started erupting from my subconscious as I was walking down the street, and I sat down on someone's stoop immediately to jot them down. It sort of signaled the start of a fairly high-energy, high-production period. For me anyway. Not for any *reasonable* writer, perhaps, but for me. And so it was an important story to me in that respect. It's still one of my favorites.

Again, as I was saying about the collaborations, "Disciples" is a story that had no place in the science fiction genre, the SF magazine market as it stood in 1981. There wasn't anybody there who would have touched it with a ten-foot pole. It did sell to PENTHOUSE, and I have to sort of give an admiring salute to the people of PENTHOUSE, Kathy Green in particular, for having the guts to publish a story this sacrilegious at a time when a lot of Moral Majority-ites and fundamentalist Christians were howling to have them driven off the newsstands altogether. There weren't any of the SF short fiction markets at the time that would've had the guts to do so. So good for them.

I was wondering how Jewish people reacted to this story?

Gardner Dozois: Except for Jack—I don't know, does *Jack* qualify as a real Jewish person? I guess he does.

I think so too.

Gardner Dozois: Well, Jack liked the story enough to buy it. I did in fact wonder if I wouldn't get as much negative reaction from Jews as from fundamentalist Christians, because I do have the Messiah coming back in the person of Murray Kupferberg from Pittsburgh. I could see where maybe some of them wouldn't like that, or would feel that I was trivializing their religious traditions or something. But I have not gotten any particular feedback on that from Jews.

I did get a little negative feedback from the Christian side, from a couple of fundamentalist Christians, but I don't recall any Jewish people complaining about the story. In fact, it was reprinted very soon after its original appearance in a book called *More Wandering Stars*, which was an anthology of science fiction and fantasy with Jewish themes edited by Jack Dann. I don't recall that any of the reviews leapt upon me in particular as being offensive or sacrilegious.

So the Jews seem to have been a good deal more tolerant about it than the Christians were on the whole. Which is probably not surprising, considering the lessons of history.

"The President of the United States sat very still in his overstuffed chair on the third floor and watched early morning sunlight sweep in a slow line across the faded rug."

In November, 1981, "Executive Clemency" appeared in OMNI, fiction editor Ellen Datlow. You wrote this with Jack Haldeman. One of my favorite stories, actually. It opens with a long, bravura description of an idiot watching the sunlight travel across the room, I'd've said quintessential Dozois, and yet you say you didn't write that?

Gardner Dozois: An idiot watching the sunlight travel across the room with the imperceptible slowness of a glacier is about as exciting as my stories ever get. Actually, my version of how this story came into being, which I thought was the real version up until the time I read Jay Haldeman's essay that he contributed to our collection *Slow Dancing Through Time*...My version was that I had gone to a Guilford writer's workshop sometime in 1973, I think, and Jay Haldeman had put a fragment of a story into the workshop—usually not a good idea, since the workshop process doesn't work well with fragments or pieces of novels in progress—but he had put a fragment into the workshop which consisted of a rough, early version of the first couple of pages of the final version of "Executive Clemency." Where the guy described as the President of the United States wakes up in the attic room of what is clearly a run-down boarding house, watches the sun creep across the floor, and shaves, and goes downstairs, and goes to where they're having breakfast and makes an inadvertent remark which everyone finds embarrassing. About how at one time Augusta did indeed have a bigger population than New York City. Although I believe in Jay's draft it was Albany rather than Augusta, but I'd have to go back to the original manuscript to check that.

The name of this fragment was "One of Our President's Brain Cells is Missing."

Not exactly a commercial title.

Gardner Dozois: Almost the first thing I did was to change the title. So it was very interesting to me. It raised a lot of questions: Why was this person calling himself the President of the United States? If he *is* the President of the United States, why is he in this shabby boarding house with these sort of run-down people? Did he just *think* that he was the President of the United States? Was this after a holocaust of some sort? There were references to New York City and so forth, and yet it seemed to be taking place in some sort of after-the-bomb scenario, where there were rural survivors. And yet the boarding house atmosphere didn't quite fit in with that either.

So there were a lot of interesting points raised by the atmosphere. I talked with Jay about this extensively, suggesting directions in which I thought the story could go. He then made what I later came to think was a big mistake, in that he said, "Well, why don't you take the story and finish it, and we'll do it as a collaboration?"

So I took it home and time went by and time went by and time went by, and about seven years later, I actually did finish the story, and we ended up selling it to OMNI.

This is what *I* thought was the story of the origin of "Executive Clemency." Jay, in *Slow Dancing Through Time*, claims that he had written the story fragment as a *parody* of my work. He had wanted to write a story fragment parody in which nothing at all happens to a character at great length, and he had done this, and I responded to it of course because I was responding to the smell of my own work buried in this parody that he had done. So I don't know.

But at any rate, I think what finally enabled me to finish this story was that I had been thinking of it—when I thought of it at all in those six or seven years—in terms that it was a story about somebody in low circumstances who thinks that he's the President of the United States. In other words, it's a delusion of grandeur that he has. He's a poor half-witted stableboy or jack-of-all-trades or whatever he is who *thinks* that he's the

President of the United States. I realized suddenly that that was wrong, that the real meat of the story was that he really *was* or had *been* the President of the United States, and he was now in these low circumstances and a half-wit. Why? How had he gotten there? What were the consequences of his being there and staying there? That started me thinking in the right direction on this story. Once I had made this fundamental epiphany, it didn't take me more than a couple of days to actually get the story into shape. I started writing I believe in the scene where he goes to see the strange wagon in front of the outriders' building, and then finished the story and then went back and reworked Jay's section, fluffing it out some, adding some more introspective psychological passages for Jamie to fluff up his characterization. Smoothing out a few things here and there. And that was basically it.

That's an interesting list of goods and services that the government man had to offer when he came to town: Paint, false teeth, eyeglasses ground to prescription, lamp oil, painless dentistry, untainted seed, flax cloth, window glass, medicines and liniment, condoms, iron farm tools, untainted livestock, nails, musical instruments, marijuana, whisky, soap, and printing done.

Gardner Dozois: I had meant that to suggest what the shape of the rest of the world beyond the borders of the town was, without actually having to get into it in any great detail. I think you get a feeling for what sort of world they're living in by seeing what sort of things they're advertising as rare and scarce items or services that you obviously can't get otherwise than by going to this thriving center of civilization that they're pushing in the story.

Is Jamie based on anybody in particular?

Gardner Dozois: No, not really. I think that this goes along with "One of Our President's Brain Cells is Missing"—I think that originally I had been thinking of him as a sort of gloating, mean-spirited caricature of Richard Nixon, down on his luck at last, and deserving every second of it. In other words, a typical liberal bugbear figure. Interestingly enough, I found that by the time I had finished this story, that the character instead had changed into one for whom you had a good deal of sympathy, and who even had an odd cracked dignity of his own. That was probably for the best as far as the story was concerned. The stories often know what you should do with them, and force you to do it whether you do yourself consciously know it or not. But I think it's a better story for the fact that Jamie, even though he was responsible for World War Three is still perceived as a sympathetic character. Rather than as some sort of mean-spirited cartoon. It probably is a better story for that.

I greatly admire the ending, where it turns out that the story is really about all the other people in the town, about small-town values. In spite of the fact that these could not have been opinions you yourself shared, when they say, "By God, he may be an idiot, but he's still the President of the United States!"

Gardner Dozois: Well, no, I don't terribly share these opinions myself, but I respect them, and there are certainly many people who have these sort of feelings, particularly people who live in small-town milieus. I have lived in small towns from time to time, and I grew up in a low-medium sized town. So to some degree I know the way in which people like this think. And I do think that under these circumstances, there would be people back in small towns in the back woods who would feel that this is still America, no matter how Balkanized and fragmented it had become, and that the President was still the President, someone to be respected, regardless of how heinously he had fucked up in the first place. And so I think that these are points of view and feelings that really do exist out there. I tried to portray them as honestly as I could, although that's probably not the way that *I* would feel under the same circumstances.

Ellen Datlow's people gave the story a really wonderful Edward Hopper painting that seemed to match the feel perfectly.

Gardner Dozois: That was one of the best illustrations I've ever had run with a story of mine, in fact, and naturally enough it was not *commissioned* for the piece. For those of you out there who have no idea who Edward Hopper is. But Hopper is one of my favorite artists anyway. Of course they didn't know that at OMNI, so it was pleasant serendipity for them to pick a Hopper piece to illustrate the story, and I do think it captured the mood of the story pretty well.

"The woods that edged the north side of Leistershire belonged to the cemetery, and if you looked westward toward Owego, you could see marble mausoleums and expensive monuments atop the hills. The cemetery took up several acres of carefully mown hillside, and bordered Jefferson Avenue, where well-kept wood-frame houses faced the rococo, painted headstones of the Italian section."

The next story was "Playing the Game," co-written with Jack Dann, which appeared in the February 1981 issue of THE TWILIGHT ZONE MAGAZINE. This is another very tricky story. Was this based on an idea you'd been carrying around for quite a while?

Gardner Dozois: In part it was and in part it wasn't. The genesis of this story was that Jack had written a three or four page fragment opening of a story that he got stuck on and didn't know what to do with, called "The Alpha Tree." Which was something about a boy who could see into alternate realities, I think. He gave this to me to work on. I sort of twisted the idea around a little bit, and altered the plot line.

The idea that once you got launched into voyages through the infinite numbers of probability worlds you could never be entirely sure that the one you were at was exactly the same as the one you started out from was an idea that had occurred to me before. So I sort of melded it in with that one. With the fragment of Jack's that was there. That's sort of where that came from.

This is another of your stories, where as soon as you learn what's going on the story's over—the ground rules have been hidden throughout the narrative.

Gardner Dozois: I had fun using some remarks which the reader takes at face value as typical literary metaphors or vague colloquialisms when passing by them the first time, but hopefully will have a new meaning when the reader goes back after finally figuring out what the story's all about. Lines, for instance, like "Things didn't change much in old town. Buildings rarely disappeared here" are taken at face value by the reader the first time through. They have quite a different meaning when you think of them in context of what is actually happening in the story, a much more literal meaning. Again, I tried to generate several statements like that in which the literal meanings were there but would not be taken that way by the reader the first time through without the knowledge of what the story's about. I would amuse myself by working several of these in.

This is a very solipsistic story. Very few people appear herein, even in reference, and those who do, the parents for instance, are infinitely mutable.

Gardner Dozois: Ahhh, I guess so. I'm not sure how deeply I really thought about the philosophic background of this, but it sort of indicates that there is a large range or spectrum of possible behaviors or personalities that any of us demonstrate. He sort of hunts around, trying to come up with a tolerable range of behavior for his parents. It can range all the way from child abuse to a sullen but tolerable social situation at home. He's learned which range he can live with, and that's the range he tries to select for.

I suppose this reflects real-life experience. I know from my own experience that you could tell often right away at breakfast what kind of a mood my father was in and how safe it was to be noticed by him on a particular day. He was often much grouchier than he was on other occasions. I suppose we all notice things like this as kids and adjust our behavior to match. So it's not really a long stretch from that to selecting which alternate set of parents you want to be with on any particular occasion.

I know you're no big fan of symbolism, but it's hard to avoid this one. Is it symbolic that he's playing his game in the cemetery, in the shadow of death? Or is this just a place you liked to hang out in as a kid?

Gardner Dozois: Well, there's several answers to that. One, yeah, the symbolism is obvious and I did nothing to downplay it. Two, the original draft of Jack's story that I was given opened up in the cemetery near the house where Jack was living at the time. I saw no particular reason to change it, since it seemed symbolically appropriate enough for what I was doing. And three, yes, I did like to hang out in cemeteries, in fact, when I was a kid. There was a big, landscaped cemetery where I used to play as a child, and it always seemed a very pastoral, unthreatening place. I was never particularly scared of it, or the fact that it contained dead bodies. I used to go there and launch little boats made out of popsicle sticks on the pond and then throw rocks at them, and pretend I was some sort of giant throwing rocks, or a catapult or something. So most of my associations with graveyards are pastoral ones rather than normal Stephen King booga-booga scary ones. That probably was there in the back of my mind too.

You'll notice that he feels safe in the graveyard. It's getting *to* the graveyard through the threatening streets where there are dogs that chase you and stuff like that that's the scary part. He's not scared in the graveyard itself.

Were there any particular problems in writing a story with just one person in it?

Gardner Dozois: No, in fact that's one of my weaknesses as a writer, that unless I make a determined effort to overcome this I *usually* end up writing stories with only one character in them. It probably is a weakness of mine as a writer. I suppose it reflects a basic self-absorption or something in that I seldom feel any tremendous need to have more than one character in my stories. I try to work more in occasionally because I do perceive this as a weakness. But the basic Dozois story, stripped to its fundamentals, will be one person in deteriorating mental or emotional condition staggering around observing a lot of stuff that's happening that he really doesn't have much to do with.

I'm aware that that's sort of the fundamental cliché Dozois story, so I try to work changes on that or avoid doing that. But that seems to be what I fall into naturally.

"I don't go to bars much—I got out of the habit when my generation was "into" sitting around in rooms with posters of Che on the wall and passing funny little cigarettes back and forth and even now that we're all middle class again, with mortgages and potbellies and expense accounts, and my idea of a pleasant evening well-spent no longer consists of listening to the same side of a Grateful Dead album thirty-five times in a row, even now I haven't really gotten back into the swing of being a barfly again."

That leads sort of naturally into "One for the Road," which appeared in the April 1982 issue of PLAYBOY and has a protagonist who encounters something awful that he can do nothing about.

Gardner Dozois: That does fit in neatly, though I must admit I wasn't thinking of that at the time I came up with the idea for the story. That was a story that forced itself upon me suddenly. I had actually been having a conversation with somebody, I forget who this was now—maybe several different people—similar to the conversation in the story, in which the question had come up, If you knew the world was going to end, would you tell anybody? And I had received a range of responses pretty similar to the range of responses I describe in the story. I was sitting and thinking about this and suddenly it occurred to me that that could be made into a story. Why I chose to cast it as a bar story I must admit I really don't remember, except that it seemed the kind of idle conversation that people would have in a bar. Perhaps that's why it started writing itself in the form of a bar story. Of course it's the kind of thing you might be told in a bar and ignore—and rightly so, ninety-nine-point-nine percent of the time. I just tried to work in an implication that this one time the story being told in a bar might have some validity behind it.

It's not a major story, by any means. I think it's competently executed. It was not meant to be a surprise ending, so much as a wry ending. And indeed I have asked a lot of people that question, and a lot of people have given me answers that fall into one or another of the categories that I list in the story. Though one person did tell me that if she knew that the world was going to come to an end in a few hours, that what she would do with the last remaining hours of her life was fly to California and punch Harlan Ellison in the mouth. To which, all I can say is, Well, to each his own.

There was a Larry Niven story where the character finds out that the world is about to come to an end, and what he wants to do is have a hot fudge sundae. So I guess there are all sorts of answers to this question.

I was working in the Franklin Institute, which is where the physicist works in the story, at the time that you wrote this. I remember I went out and figured out that this must be the Cherry Street Tavern that it was set in, because it was the only bar that fit the parameters. Was this so?

Gardner Dozois: No, actually, I just figured there must be a bar somewhere near the Franklin Institute, so I just made one come into existence. I didn't do any research as to bars in the vicinity of the Franklin Institute. Which is not actually named in the story. I was a little cagier than that. The city is not specified, nor what Institute it is that the physicist is working at.

It sold to PLAYBOY, too. You were selling a lot of fiction to PLAYBOY at that time.

Gardner Dozois: Well, it's a PLAYBOY sort of story. Short, snappy, with a wry sort of twist ending. Not particularly deep. Nothing tremendously controversial. But amusing, and glibly handled. I tried to work a twist on the bar stories that I was familiar with, a minor twist, in having the character be an old hippie doper who wasn't particularly enthusiastic about bars, but found himself in one anyway. That's not much of a twist, but considering the range of bar stories, that's not bad.

"Have you ever toured the Harding Dam in Boulder, Colorado? Have you ever caught that old Errol Flynn movie about the life of Lord Bolingbroke, the man who restored the Stuarts to the British throne and overran half of France but who 'couldn't conquer the Queen he didn't dare to love,' a real classic, also starring Basil Rathbone and Olivia de Havilland? Have you?"

That's the second story to come out in 1982. The third story was a collaboration, "Snow Job," which appeared in HIGH TIMES, of all places.

Gardner Dozois: Yes, appeared in an issue of HIGH TIMES with a girlie-magazine-like gatefold of a marijuana plant. I guess for everyone who wants to masturbate while looking at a marijuana plant. I suppose somewhere there must be a doper hard-core and dedicated enough to do this, but I don't think I ever met the fellow.

This story was originally the opening story of a novel I was going to write, and you were giving me advice on it. Then I discovered that I was never going to write it, and about a

year later you decided to turn it into an entirely different story.

Gardner Dozois: I must admit, as I think I said in the introduction in *Slow Dancing Through Time*, that this was basically a stunt. I'm very thrifty by nature, especially where stories are concerned, and I have a horror of wasting material that you don't get some use out of by publishing. Never throw anything away, have scraps of stories that go back for years. Which occasionally I will find some use for and will throw them into the meld for some new story that's underway.

I happened to be looking through your opening chapter one day, and I said to myself, Gee, there's a lot of good material here. This coke scam scene, which is very long, is very well detailed, and it's a shame to waste this, because all it needs is a different rationale for why the coke scam is happening. It could function as part of a completely different story.

At first I thought for a minute or two that maybe you needed to salvage it for use in some sort of mainstream or mystery story. But then I quickly decided that would be hard to sell, and I suddenly saw a way that it could be made to function as part of a science fiction story instead. And I thought that considering that we're in the business that would be much easier to sell than a mystery mainstream coke scam story. I saw that indeed all you needed was some plot armature at the beginning and the end to justify why he was there doing the coke scam, and the coke scam scene could function almost without any changes, almost as written. The science fiction rationale and the plot armature could be added at either end without altering the internal mechanics at all. You sort of wrap a science fiction story around the detailed coke scam scene, and that's what I proceeded to do. I just had to think of some rationale for why this scam could function as part of a science fiction story, and once I started to think of it in those terms it wasn't difficult to come up with one. I merely added the science fiction plot at the beginning to get him into the coke scam scene, and then at the end to wrap up what had happened after the scene, and made into rather a neat package, I think.

It's startling to me how seamlessly the story reads considering that, as you say, you didn't change any of the middle. You just layered an entirely different plot onto it.

Gardner Dozois: I took particular care to feather over the joins between the beginning and the end and the middle, so as to make the transition as little jarring as possible.

You open with a description of Hollywood movie that most of us have never seen, an alternate timeline movie. Was this an idea you had stuffed away in a back drawer?

Gardner Dozois: No, not really, I must admit. Soon as I determined that it was going to be a time-travel story and that it was going to be a changing reality time-travel story, I then had to come up with some examples of how reality had been altered in ways that we as innocent civilians would not suspect. I don't know why the movie came to mind. Perhaps I had been watching old Errol Flynn movies on the late show or something. It just seemed like a good example. If history had been changed in this way, they probably *would* have made a bad, inaccurate Hollywood movie about it. It probably would've had Erroll Flynn in it. It just seemed like a good example of the sort of thing I was looking for.

No particular significance, I don't think.

It was hard coming up with scams that *could* have changed history that are well enough known that people would understand what I was talking about. The Teapot Dome scandal, I think, was one that we came up with, and the thing with the Errol Flynn movie was another. But there aren't too many that you could just mention and have people say, "Oh, yeah." In fact

I was glad I had Watergate to save for the stinger at the end because I don't know what I would've used otherwise that would've had any sort of "Oh, yeah," type of impact on people.

Because the fact is that most of the audience is not very familiar with history, which is a problem with alternate history stories. I've read several at work recently that are very intricately detailed but the history that they turn on is obscure enough that nobody is going to understand what the point of the story is. Which is a problem when you're writing alternate history stories in this day of functional illiteracy.

I should ask you—*Were* you surprised when you came in the door and were handed a completely different story?

My mouth fell open. I came in and you said, "Wait till I finish typing this," and you finished typing a paragraph, put the manuscript together, handed it to me and said, "Congratulations, you've just written a story." I was sure this was some kind of obscure New Wave joke. One thing I did know was that I had *not* just written a story. So when you put it in my hand, it really did feel like somebody had just shifted reality from underneath me. Appropriately enough.

"Bruckman first discovered that Wernecke was a vampire when they went to the quarry that morning."

The heavy-hitter of 1982 was "Down Among the Dead Men," which you and Jack wrote and which appeared in the July issue of OUI. That's a pretty grim story, and as far as we know that's the first vampire in the Holocaust story, isn't it?

Gardner Dozois: I think that it was. Although apparently there have been a number of them subsequently, which I am not really familiar with. Some critic made a comment in reviewing that story that it was the first of the flood of the vampire in the Holocaust stories. I must admit I haven't read any of the other ones.

I don't remember what gave me the idea for the story. I do know that it existed as a sentence in my story idea notebook for several years, until I was talking about potential story ideas with Jack at one point, and threw this story idea out. I believe the form it exists in my notebook, I'd have to check, is "Vampire in Nazi death camp in World War II." That was really all we had to work with.

Talking about alternate histories, my memory is that I mentioned this idea to Jack and that he was initially very enthusiastic about it, and went and sat down at my typewriter and started writing it after we had discussed it for a few minutes. Jack's memory is that I had mentioned this idea and that he had dismissed it and was very reluctant to do anything with it, and that I had to convince him that it would be a good idea to write this story. Now, which one of these versions is correct, no one will ever know at this point, I guess, unless hidden tapes of conversations in my apartment show up in my FBI file or something in the future.

At any rate, what's beyond doubt is that after we discussed it for a while, Jack sat down to the typewriter and wrote ferociously for at least a couple of hours, and roughed out the opening part of the story through the opening Passover scene, and then stopped and left I think for Binghamton the next day. I took over the story after the Passover scene and continued it from there. We worked out some story problems later in the manuscript and passed a couple of drafts of the final scene back and forth.

Fundamentally, the first nine or ten pages of the manuscript are Jack's.

Once again, when feathering over the join, I tried to feather it over as seamlessly as possible. One way I did this, and this is true of "Snow Job" as well, is I went back into the material that Jack had written by himself, some paragraphs before where I actually took over and dropped in a couple of sentences that were in a style more like mine and less like his. To sort of ease the transition from one section to the other, so there wouldn't be a stylistic lurch there where we switched from one author to the other. That was one way I tried to feather over the join there.

We also had a slight disagreement about the ending of the story. I prefer it to end with the line "His mouth filled with the strong, clean taste of copper." Which is the way I reprinted it in *Slow Dancing Through Time*. Jack prefers the final paragraph that appears after that in I think the *Blood is Not Enough* reprinting. Which shows what's happening the next day. I thought that was unnecessary because I thought that everything that's shown in that final paragraph was implicit in the situation where he's drinking Wernecke's blood the night before.

So I left it off. When he reprints it in his collection, he can put the paragraph back on if he wants. It shows you that things are always fluid. There's never 100% agreement on these things.

That was a pretty outrageous story to think you could get away with. *I* would've been hesitant in Jack's place. Did you get any negative feedback on that?

Gardner Dozois: We got some negative feedback. Some people said it was in bad taste. One very well known horror writer whose name I will not mention, but whose own work is fairly gory, said that it was the most morally offensive story that he had ever read. And in fact I believe canceled or threatened to cancel his F&SF subscription because of the tastelessness of this particular story. Which considering some of the stuff that this person has written himself I found a little odd.

But generally the response has been fairly favorable. There's some negative responses. Some people thought it was in bad taste, as I said, but on the whole most people thought it was a fairly powerful story. I think perhaps why we got away with it without getting more negative response than we did is that it's not played for cheap shock value. It's played in a more sober, somber way than that. It's not played for shock effect. And also the vampire in a way is a victim too. He's struggling to survive, just as all the other people in the camp are struggling to survive. It's not a situation that he particularly desires to be in, and in fact it's a situation that is dangerous to him. Perhaps more so to him than for the rest of the inmates.

It boils down to the question of identity. Which is an irony that I like, in that even though he is a vampire he is perceived by the Nazis to be a Jew and so that's the way they treat him. Like a Jew, no better or worse than they treat any of the other Jews. And again there is an irony in that he *is* helping some of his fellow inmates to survive even at the same time as he is also taking blood from them, taking life from them. So there is an intended irony there as well. It perhaps says something about the wider human situation in addition to just the situation of the camps.

Did you do a lot of research on the Holocaust for this story?

Gardner Dozois: Jack of course had already written a story about the Holocaust, his story "Camps," which takes place in a death camp. So he had already done research, which showed up in the opening section which he wrote himself. I myself read a couple of books on the Holocaust before going on to write the rest of the story, to get some of the details right, and then of course I consulted with Jack on some of it.

It's a moderately accurate view of the camps, I think.

"There were four of them who entered the haunted darkness of the Old Forest that night, but only three who would return because three was a magic number."

The final story of 1982, "The Sacrifice," appeared in F&SF, a small piece about Featherflower the unicorn. How did you come to write this?

Gardner Dozois: Again it's a fairly ignoble or base reason to write a story, but I'd been doing intensive research on unicorns for my anthology with Jack, my unicorn anthology. I'd been reading a lot of unicorn stories, this is probably what primed the pump subconsciously. And I realized that what I couldn't find and what apparently didn't exist, to my surprise, was a simple basic reversal of the unicorn legend. In other words, where they staked the unicorn out somewhere, and the human laid itself out at the unicorn's feet, rather than the other way around. As soon as this occurred to me, I saw the scene, and I immediately opened my notebook and wrote the basic scene down, where the human appears at the end.

Having done this I then realized that the only way the story would work was if I disguised as well as I could the fact that all the characters in it were unicorns until the last paragraph of the story. So the rest of the story was an exercise in misdirection. Again, trying to play fair with the descriptions of what was happening, but at the same time manipulate the language in such a way that the fact that they were unicorns would not be given away, and wouldn't become obvious until in retrospect, when the human crashes out through the trees.

It's a minor little piece of fluff. If I hadn't thought suddenly of how to work the last paragraph where the human actually appears to the unicorn and written it down, I probably never would have bothered to go and do the two or three page buildup to this.

I deliberately made the names clichéd in a special sort of way. I wanted clichéd names that would be acceptable as names for unicorns once you realized they were unicorns but that when you first came across them, on first reading the story, would seem like the kind of clichéd names that primitive people often have in science fiction or fantasy stories. That was why I selected the names that I selected.

I hardly think this was the finest hour of Western literature. It was an amusing little idea that had occurred to me, and I was feeling energetic at the time so I tossed it off.

There's a good side and a down side to being in a fairly high creative energy period. Ideas of this sort occur to me all the time but when I'm not in a high energy cycle I don't actually bother to put in the effort to do anything with them. When I *am* in high creative energy cycle I do sometimes put in the effort to do something with them. The good news then is that you end up with some extra stories. The bad news, though, is that they're not necessarily the most significant or worthwhile stories that ever existed.

Still, I don't suppose that it really did any fundamental harm to the state of Western civilization that this story appeared in F&SF. So I guess I'm not all that ashamed of it when you come right down to it.

How much time did it take you to write it?

Gardner Dozois: Oh, maybe a day.

Is there anything more you can think to add before we move on to the next story?

Gardner Dozois: No, not really. Except that doing these fantasy theme anthologies has taught me that a lot of the fundamental changes you would think would have been worked on these themes decades ago have in fact actually never been done by anyone. So there's still a lot of work that could be done in filling out some of these themes.

"Later, waking from uneasy dreams, he had been afraid that the world was about to be switched off."

We're up to 1983 now. "A Traveler in an Antique Land" was published in *Chrysalis 10*, edited by Roy Torgeson. This is an older piece than other stories published at about the same time. What's the history of this?

Gardner Dozois: This was a story I started writing pieces of while I was in London in 1969. I wrote it pretty much the same time that I was writing "Horse of Air," while I was in Europe. Written mostly in a notebook while I was sitting out at various sidewalk cafes and other romantic-sounding milieus.

It was finished sometime in '69 before I returned to the States. I made a couple of abortive attempts to sell it but of course since it's not really a science fiction story it found little receptivity and it pretty much sat in my files for many years. Until I finally sold it to Roy Torgeson who for some reason, I'm still not entirely sure why, bought it for his *Chrysalis* series.

This I don't think is a tremendously successful piece overall. I think again that it has some good bits of writing in it. I wrote the bulk of it in London in fragmented fashion and then when I returned a couple of weeks later to Germany I tidied it up and added some stuff and tied it together. I don't think it's entirely successful. It was my attempt to do a sort of an "I Am A Camera" sort of scenario where most of the feelings and impressions and things that I saw in England I transmogrified to some degree as fiction and wrote down in this story. Which doesn't have a plot *per se.*

The problem is that being the sort of person that I was and given the position I was in in London, nothing tremendously interesting happened to me. So as a result there's nothing tremendously interesting in the story. If I had gone to decadent, wild sex-orgies, where people were swinging from trapezes while having sex with goats and shooting up drugs through their nostrils it probably would've been more interesting. But unfortunately none of that happened to me. So none of it is in the story.

I think there are a couple of interesting sensory impressions of London here and there in the story. But that's obviously not enough to really make it function successfully as an organic piece.

There was sort of a vague attempt here at a mosaic effect in that these little glittery mosaic pieces were supposed to add up subliminally across to being more than the sum of their parts. But I don't think that actually works.

With this experiment I pretty much decided that it wasn't enough just to put down on paper everything that happened to you. You needed the organized focus of art. You needed plot. You needed characters. You needed a theme. The raw stuff of your life put down on paper was not sufficiently intriguing enough to function as art. Artifice was needed. Craft was needed.

Actually that's a little bit unfair to my younger self, since there is some artifice and craft here. But once again it's buried too far below the surface for you really to be able to expect that the reader is going to get anything out of it in particular.

This is obviously a very autobiographical piece. A couple of the characters here look like they might be people who

science fiction readers would recognize. There's a character here who's driving too fast on the wrong side of the road, talking about his sex life, for example. He must have been in the science fiction community.

Gardner Dozois: That's very perceptive of you. Actually, there is no one here who has later become famous to my knowledge. But many of the people described herein were based on people I had met in science fiction fan circles in England in '68 and '69 when I was going to my first two conventions. Which were the British convention Eastercon in '68 and '69. I had become friendly with some British fans. The Hartfordshire fan club in fact, I went to a meeting of in '69. Many of the people described here are people from that fan group. Or friends of mine from my army days. There are a couple of old friends of mine from my army days who are described in here since they did indeed go over to England with me at one point. But nobody as far as I know in here actually became a famous personage. Although I believe that one or two of them are still active in science fiction fandom to one degree or another. But there's no famous writer disguised thinly in here to my knowledge.

They weren't famous writers at the time, anyway.

Was the letter from the friend in Viet Nam a real letter? Or was that an invention?

Gardner Dozois: Well, it was an invention, but it was an invention based on material from my own life. I did have a fairly close friend in the army who was rotated in Viet Nam. Actually, let me see that—I haven't looked at this story in about fifteen years.

No, actually the text of the letter is real. Sorry. Looking at it again. The text is from a letter I received from a friend who was rotated from Germany to Viet Nam. We received this letter and then I never heard from him again. Subsequent attempts to get in contact with him failed, and I can only assume that he probably was killed.

This obviously affected me on an emotional level since it was a totally random process. The rotation levy came through our office and happened to take him rather than one of the others of us. But it could just as easily have taken me. Again, sort of indicates the random nature of the universe. As I think the character muses therein, some people get to sit in sidewalk cafes and drink coffee and write in their notebooks, and some of them get to have their chest shot out and die in the mud, and it's hard to see what the factors there are that single one out to have one happen to them instead of the other.

There's a strong hint of circularity in the story. It begins with the protagonist waking from uneasy dreams, and ends, "As he slept, the sky darkened and the wind began to rise." At the risk of analyzing this, there are only two ways to read it, and one is that at the end of the story he goes back to the beginning, and the other is that at the beginning of the story he has a premonition of catastrophe at the end.

Gardner Dozois: This is what craft and artifice do exist in the story manifesting itself. As I said, it wasn't entirely that I just put everything that happened to me down with no hint of an organizing principle. There was a vague, artsy organizing principle in my mind when I actually assembled all this material. The circularity is intentional. I had also intended that you could read it either way. That either he was waking where the story begins, or that doom was hurtling towards them. I think that either reading is valid from the text.

There is a sort of encroaching apocalyptic subtext which I scattered here and there throughout the text. Mainly consisting of racial and social strife in the society. Since at the time that I was over there, there was indeed a lot of increasing racial tension. It seemed possible that we would end up with a racial warfare situation of the sort that I described as happened in the United States in other stories.

The story probably would have been the better for it if I had actually included this as an overt plot rather than as a sort of subliminal mosaic patterning subtext behind the scenes. But it's certainly possible, and I believe valid, to read these all as premonitions of social apocalypse. In fact I think he has a dream or vision of social apocalypse at some point in the story. So you could read that as a foreshadowing of the reality that he's going to wake into when he wakes at the end of the story.

To that extent there is a plot of sorts. I don't think it really works. I had intended it to function as a plot without actually having to have a plot and I think that this probably was not the best decision that I could have made. There are many little thematic touches there that hook up with each other, and I had intended them to give the text a sort of an underlying resonance, an underlying continuity.

I think that the story sort of got hung up between being an autobiographical recasting of things that I saw and being fiction, and I think that it's uneasily hung up thereby. I probably should have just strengthened the fictional elements and made it actual fiction without being constrained by what actually had happened to me in reality. I didn't put anything in—with the exception of the dreams that he has, I didn't put anything into the text that didn't actually happen to me or that I didn't actually see in reality. And I think that that was a constraint I set for myself arbitrarily that in a way sort of misses the point of fiction.

What is interesting is not what *actually* happened to me, but what I could have imagined *might* have happened to me. That is what I should really have written down, instead of accepting the constraint that only things I had actually seen or experienced myself, however transmogrified they are, were going to go into the story. So I think the story as it exists is sort of half one thing and half the other without being entirely successful as either. As I said, nothing interesting enough really happened to me to make it successful as an interesting piece of autobiography. And the fictional elements that do exist in the text are not brought up strongly enough to make it function strongly enough as fiction to be successful. It sort of falls between two stools, and as a result I don't think it's successful as either.

Although there are a couple of interesting touches here and there. A couple of worthwhile passages. I don't think it really works as I had intended it to work.

"Jesus Christ appeared at Kess Kimbrough's door dressed in a white tuxedo with a blue cummerbund and matching bow-tie. His chestnut-brown hair was parted in the middle and fell down past his shoulders, and his beard and mustache were close-cropped and neatly combed."

"Slow Dancing With Jesus" appeared in the July 1983 issue of PENTHOUSE. Kathy Green was the fiction editor. You wrote this in collaboration with Jack Dann and it's unique in that you had very little input into the plot.

Gardner Dozois: That's true. The plot was pretty much fixed by the time we sat down to write the story. What had happened, as I tell in my introduction to the story in *Slow Dancing Through Time*, is that my friend Tess Kissinger has weird dreams, very vivid and imaginative, and one day she told me about this dream that she'd had, when in high school, an unpopular teenager in high school, that Jesus had taken her to the prom and all the kids were very impressed with this. And Jesus had said, "She's with me, and if she's with me you *know* she's cool." This had really blown everybody away in her dream.

I thought this was a great dream and I saw potentials immediately that this could be turned into a story. And I sort of hinted at her for a year or so that she ought to write it. But this didn't seem to really register with her. She didn't take the possibility seriously. So she never did get around to writing it. I even hinted at her at one point—and I think you were there as a witness to this, Michael—that maybe we should do this as a collaboration.

I remember that.

Gardner Dozois: But this hint didn't hit upon fertile ground either. So nothing happened with this. A year or so went by. And we went to dinner with Jack Dann, I believe at Dave Shorer's restaurant. Jack Dann was there, Tess's boyfriend, the artist Bob Walters, was there, and Susan was there. We were having dinner and something in the conversation—I forget exactly what the turn was—but something in the conversation reminded me of this and I had her relate her Jesus at the Prom dream to Jack. And Jack, being much more aggressive than I, leapt forward with a shout of "Oh boy, what a great story *this* would make!" And immediately assumed that he and I were going to write this as a collaboration and started making plans to do so. We then finished dinner. He did ask Tess if we could write it. She was somewhat dazed and said yes. I'm not sure how seriously she took all of this. We then got in a taxi cab and went home. When we got home, Jack sat down at a typewriter and started writing it.

I must say that if I been working on the story by myself it probably would never have gotten written. Because already in the taxi cab on the way home I was having cold feet about how difficult it would be to pull it off. But Jack just plunged right in and turned out a couple of pages. So I was sort of committed at that point to do something with it. The major thing I wanted to do with it was to not have it merely be a sacrilegious joke like a Monty Python sketch. That would have been the easy way to handle it. But I wanted something that was a little more ambitious than that. I thought that the interesting thing was not the sacrilegious joke part but the fact that it arose out of a young girl's longing dreams. That was the quality that had to be brought to the story. That was the quality I then tried to bring subsequently to writing my part of it. Not just that Jesus was taking her to the prom, blackout, big yuck, but that there was a drifting, bittersweet sort of quality to it. That was the quality I tried to infuse in it.

Did it take long to write?

Gardner Dozois: It didn't really take very long to write. I believe that Jack had written the first couple of pages taking us up to the point where they actually arrive at the prom outside the high school building. I took it from there. It only took a couple of days—maybe three days—to write after that. I would have to look it up on my calendar to be sure. But it was very delicate work because I felt like you were threading your way through a mine field in a way. In that any careless phrase or sentence could shatter the very delicate mood of the story that I was trying to create and dump it back into being just a sacrilegious joke, and I don't think it would have worked that way. It needed that dreamlike, lyrical, bittersweet quality. Because it *was* arising from a young girl's dreams about acceptance and love and so forth. And that was what I thought needed to be done with it. I think that was the direction it needed to be taken in. So I was fairly careful in how it was phrased. I tried to treat Jesus at the same time as being a cool, sporty figure and yet there was a fairly reverential tone to the way he was handled. There were a lot of obvious jokes and shticks I could have gone for that I did not. Because Jesus basically has to be taken seriously as an archetype within the dream even though he's cool and he's driving a sports car and he's winking jauntily at people. Still, at base the reason this works is because he's Jesus, an archetypically potent figure. And if he's not treated with respect as an archetypically potent figure then he doesn't serve the function that he ought to serve in the mechanics of the plot.

Although I did have one fundamentalist Christian chide me for using Jesus in this way, I think primarily it was a respectful utilization of him because, without getting into whether I believe in Jesus as a divine figure or not, I was treating his archetype with respect and using his archetype as an archetypically potent mythic figure. Even though the satirical elements were there, as I say I didn't want it just to be a Monty Python sacrilegious joke. I don't think it would've had any power if it was just that because that's not where the power in the dream lay. The power of the dream was not just that Jesus took her to the prom but that Jesus took her to the prom and this convinced everybody else that she was cool. So in order for that to have happened, Jesus must be a potent figure mythologically.

It's kind of ironic that this story appeared in PENT-HOUSE.

Gardner Dozois: Well, indeed, I don't know where it *would* have appeared if it didn't appear in PENTHOUSE. Everybody told me that we would never sell the story. My agent told me we would never sell it, and everybody said it was just about impossible to sell. It was too weird, a bit more satiric than was the norm, it was too short, it was sacrilegious, it had a woman as the viewpoint character. It was about grungy high school kids instead of brand-name consuming affluent yuppies. It was all wrong for the slicks in particular. We never expected we would sell it to the slicks. But indeed we did, on the second crack out of the gate. Somewhat to my surprise.

I really do have to be respectful of PENTHOUSE for taking

it at that particular time because it was a controversial, sacrilegious—could be *interpreted* as a sacrilegious story. Although that's not the way *I* see it.

And they were taking it at a time when PENTHOUSE was under heavy fire from the Moral Majority people and Jesse Helms and it looked like the government was going to do its best to get them banned from the newsstands altogether. So it took a certain amount of guts to publish a story like that at that particular time. They also within a year or so published my in some ways even riskier solo story, "Disciples," which also had a sacrilegious element in it or could be so interpreted. So you have to respect them for taking a chance with this kind of material at a time when they had a lot to lose.

If they hadn't published it I don't know who would have published it. I doubt it would have sold to the SF magazines of the day. It's possible that Shawna McCarthy might have bought it a few years later at ASIMOV'S, but again it's possible nobody *ever* would have bought it. So, who knows?

You have one instant that's right on the edge, when Jesus kisses her goodnight and there's a "sweet hint of tongue."

Gardner Dozois: Yeah, that was a little on the edge. I also thought I skirted a little bit on the edge with the last line of the story, which is actually, the tone of the rest of the story, when she writes in the diary, "Dear Diary, Tonight I met...Him," with the H capitalized. But it *was* a satirical story after all, so I felt I could allow myself a couple of—you'll excuse the expression—satirical *licks* here and there as long as I handled the tone of the rest of the story right. It was important to establish a sad, melancholy, bittersweet mood in the rest of the story and then I think you can get away with the bright satirical licks here and there, and it still would do what I wanted it to do. At least I hope that it did.

"Roy had dreamed of the sea, as he often did. When he woke up that morning, the wind was sighing through the trees outside with a sound like the restless murmuring of surf, and for a moment he thought that he was home, back in the tidy brick house by the beach, with everything that had happened undone, and hope opened hotly inside him, like a wound."

The next story was "The Peacemaker," which appeared in the August 1983 ASIMOV'S under Shawna McCarthy. That was your first Nebula, and a cover story, and all in all a pretty successful story for you.

Gardner Dozois: This actually taught me a lesson I don't think was at all surprising, that although I'd had several stories up for Nebulas and awards in years past, it was the first story I'd had that was the cover story of a genre digest science fiction magazine that actually *won* the award. That pretty much taught me that if you want to win awards in science fiction, you'd better publish in the genre science fiction magazines. I think subsequent events have indicated that for the most part that's more or less true.

   Of course in a way it was a moot lesson, since most of the stuff that I had been writing was unacceptable to most of the genre science fiction magazines until about that point in the eighties. So it wasn't as if I was sneeringly refusing to sell my stories to the genre digest magazines. It was that for the most part they weren't interested in them. Which is what forced me into the original anthologies of the seventies that published the bulk of my work up until that point, and also in an odd way into the slicks since the genre digest magazines weren't interested in most of our collaborations either. Which ended up then going to places like OMNI, PENTHOUSE, PLAYBOY, and even HIGH TIMES, places that were more receptive to a degree of weirdness that wasn't washing in the genre market at that point.

So as I say it did teach me a lesson. If you want to get exposure you go for the digest SF magazines. On the other hand that's all very well as long as the digest magazines are willing to buy your stuff you want exposure for in the first place. Which by and large they had not been up until that point. So it was an important story for me in that it saw me getting a little more acceptance within the genre digest market where I hadn't had a *lot* of penetration to that day. An occasional story here and there. I'd had a couple in AMAZING and even one in ANALOG, strangely enough, which had actually won the Anlab for that month. But I think "The Peacemaker" really represented me being accepted more by the digest magazine market to some extent.

The premise behind it is that one day the oceans rise. The ice caps or a large portion of the ice caps melt. At the time you said this was actually a possible scenario. How much research did you do?

Gardner Dozois: I did a moderate amount of research for me. Not being a really hard science writer type of person I don't tend to do years of research for short stories. I had read a couple of articles about this sort of "marine transgression," as it's called, including an article—I could find the derivation for you if I looked for it—from NATURAL HISTORY magazine, which I read every so often, about this very sort of thing having happened in the past. And indeed there's fairly good evidence that the sea levels have gone up by a couple of hundred feet in the past with relative speed. It's obviously nothing that couldn't happen. The only controversial point was whether it would happen as fast as the story indicates that it would or whether it would go up by a matter of inches over a period of decades. I personally think that the evidence that it could go up that fast is fairly solid if you look at the historical record. It may be something that we all have to worry about in the future if global warming is really the real thing. It may well be something we all have to worry about.

I did sit down with a contour map of the United States and plot out as carefully as I could where the new coastlines would fall if the sea level came up a couple of hundred feet and you'd lose most of the areas that I say you would lose. You even lose some surprising areas inland because of things like the sea would transgress down the St. Lawrence River and you'd lose a lot of the areas in the middle that were low ground. Because the sea could reach them that way. This isn't really surprising, though, since most of the interior, the Midwest, of the United States was ocean until a few million years back, before the glaciers.

It's one very real possibility. Scientists can't seem to entirely come to a consensus as to whether we're going to be faced with a greenhouse-effect, global warming future where the ice caps melt and the sea level comes up or an ice age future where we've got glaciers grinding down on us. There's actually evidence for both scenarios and nobody seems to have really decided which one is true, although the consensus of opinion seems to be swinging slowly toward the global warming scenario.

Even if it doesn't happen as fast as it happens in the story—which I do think is possible—it would certainly be a major social problem. Even if it came up at the rate of a few feet a decade it could be a major social problem that would eventually demand the relocation of cities and the shifting of much of our industrial base. Since almost all of our major cities in fact are built on ground low enough to be affected. Most of New Jersey for instance is only a couple of feet above sea level, so a rise of even a couple of feet in the sea level would pretty much put the sea at least up to Philadelphia and perhaps further inland depending on how much of a rise it had been. Or else it'd take out most of Florida. Just to name a few examples. It could be quite nasty.

"The man-who-wasn't-there first spoke to Marcy when she was eight years old."

Your next story was "Time Bride," which you wrote with Jack Dann, and which appeared in PLAYBOY in December, 1983. Who came up with this idea?

Gardner Dozois: *I* came up with the idea, although of course it's just a variant on the long sub-genre of time-viewer stories. The spark that got me interested was the thought that there were certain areas of life that are usually *not* being spied on by people from the future in these stories, although that very area certainly *would* be spied on by anyone who actually *had* such a time-viewer. And I saw interesting potentials for conflict there. It may have been my idea, but it was Jack who actually started *writing* the story. With his usual Jack-like enthusiasm and energy, he plunged in and wrote most of the second scene in the story, which was actually the first thing to be put down on paper. The scene where the voice is speaking to Mr. Meisner from the ceiling? Which comes after the long opening section, which I added later. The story at the time opened with the voice addressing the girl's father from the ceiling and him going through the shtick of saying "Is this God?" and so forth. That whole scene was Jack's pretty much in total. I later went back and added the opening section where the girl is playing by herself, after picking Susan's brains for games that she played in her childhood, which I inserted into the story before the ceiling-talking scene, the original opener; the idea was to show the idyllic nature of her childhood before Arnold came along, and to provide an evocative, wistful tone to contrast with the jokier tone of the next section—and so I could add other lyrical scenes later on in the story without it being so much of a jar with the other scenes; the story *starts* out lyrical and somber, so it doesn't throw you out when you hit that later..

As I recall the story, it goes from that opening section to the section where Mr. Meisner is being talked to by the time traveler, and then it goes into the scenes where the deal that they strike is in effect.

The opening section in which she's playing a jump rope game—"Mimsy, clapsy, I whirl my hands to bapsie," and so on—is very reminiscent of Avram Davidson's first story, "My Boy Friend's Name is Jello." I wonder if you were thinking of that specifically, or if it's just part of the diffuse influence every significant writer has on those writers who come after.

Gardner Dozois: Actually, that whole line I got whole cloth out of Susan's childhood; apparently this *was* the jump rope chant or ball-playing chant they actually used when they were kids. So perhaps *they* were influenced by Avram Davidson back in the fifties; more likely Avram Davidson stole real jump-rope chants for his story too—which, in fact, I believe he said was the case.

The basic idea-thread here was that the girl was being saved by the guy from the future to be the perfect bride for him, and the only way she could get *out* of having him watch her all the time was to lose her virginity and prove herself to be an unworthy slut as quickly as she could. The sequence near the end, where she sneaks out of the house on a mission to lose her virginity, was a scene which I wrote early on, before many of the earlier sections were written. Then we went back afterward and retrofitted in some of those sequentially earlier scenes.

Most of the "intervention" scenes, where Arnold is nagging Marcy about not eating lobster and so forth, were written by Jack, with little if any input from me. Most of the scenes dealing with Marcy when she's by herself were written by me.

And then of course at the end, for the twist ending, her life has been ruined by this experience, and the only way that she can find any joy is to get one of these machines herself and go back and persecute her persecutor when he was a child. Was that in there from the beginning, and has her persecution of him caused him to grow up into the kind of person who would persecute her? Or has the plot shifted off into another paradoxical timeline?

Gardner Dozois: It's a tail-swallower, of course. I am not sure whether I intended that ending when I was writing the bulk of the story. But by the time I finished the story, it had become clear that it needed an extra twist at the ending. Particularly in the market we were aiming for, which was the men's magazines.

Just freeing Marcie from persecution wouldn't make for a very satisfying story.

Gardner Dozois: I think my original instinct was to end with having her free herself from his persecution by getting herself laid. But it occurred to me by the time I had finished the story, that that wasn't really enough of a twist. So I had her going out and getting a time machine herself. Later on, at the request of Shawna McCarthy, I fluffed that ending out some, and added more detail, and toned the sex scene down a bit for publication in ASIMOV'S; it had earlier been published in PLAYBOY; the version in *Slow Dancing Through Time* included details from both drafts.

It's actually a very dark ending, because, of course, she's perpetuating the "chain of blows," as it's been called. Her childhood was ruined so she's going to ruin somebody else's childhood, even if it *is* the guy who originally ruined hers. So it's all passed along. The negativity is passed along from one generation to another. There's usually not a causal loop involved in the real world, but the chain of blows is very real, where the child is mistreated and so mistreats his or her own children when they have the chance.

It would have been much more karmically healthy if she had *broken* the chain of blows, and decided to forgive Arnold instead, or at least ignore him. But, unfortunately, that doesn't make for as snappy an ending, so that was not the way it worked.

"The old house had been hit by something sometime during the war and mashed nearly flat. The front was caved in as though crushed by a giant fist: wood pulped and splintered, beams protruding at odd angles like broken fingers, the second floor collapsed onto the remnants of the first. The rubble of a chimney covered everything with a red mortar blanket. On the right, a gaping hole cross-sectioned the ruins, laying bare all the strata of fused stone and plaster and charred wood—everything curling back on itself like the lips of a gangrenous wound. Weeds swarmed up the low hillside from the road and swept over the house, wrapping the ruins in wildflowers and grapevines, softening the edges of destruction with green."

Let's move on to "Morning Child." Which appeared in OMNI in January, 1984 and won you a Nebula Award. So this cannot be an entirely unpleasant story to talk about.

Gardner Dozois: It's a story that shows you the value of never throwing anything away.

Really!

Gardner Dozois: Yes. Young writers should take a lesson from this. I had written the opening scene of that story—the first two or three pages of the story—oh, maybe fifteen, twenty years before I actually wrote the rest of the story.

I had written the scene when I was living in Milford, Pennsylvania, which is clearly recognizable as the place where the story is set, if you've ever been to Milford, Pennsylvania. I had written a scene of an old man and a young boy visiting the ruins of what is clearly Damon Knight's old house, the Anchorage, and harvesting day lilies and other edible roots and then walking back along the highway to roughly where I myself lived when I was in Milford. Obviously the world had been ruined in some sort of catastrophe, and, in fact, the original idea was that this was going to be an After-The-Bomb story, showing how the man and his son survived in a Post-Holocaust world.

I couldn't figure out what to do with it after the opening scene, so I stopped about three pages in and put it away. And then, many years later, I was flipping idly through my files— one of several times this has happened to me—and looked at the old fragment again, and suddenly I saw what I could do with it. So I finished it, incorporating the old pages, adding some new paragraphs to them interstitially, and going on to finish the rest of the story.

I think the difference was that in the interval, several days before flipping through my files, I had a dream...which is hard to describe, as most dreams are. But which *did* feature a sort of a time-shifting effect, where people in the dream were growing old and then young again, sort of at random. So that one minute you'd be talking to someone and he'd be an old man, and the next minute you'd be talking to him and he would be a child. I got up that morning and I made a note of that somewhere.

So that was on my mind when I was examining that fragment again, and I suddenly saw that you could use that time-shifting idea, almost like being a werewolf except that what changes is your age, rather than your shape...I saw that I could use that concept in this particular fragment.

Now when I had written this story originally, the old man was just an old man and the child was just a child. But I saw that I could play some tricky games here by having the child age during the course of the story. Most of the effort that went into the story was trying to keep the reader from realizing before I wanted them to realize what actually was going on. So I tried to phrase things very ambiguously, so that the reader would take it on face value the first time through, but then, in retrospect, it would be clear that I had meant *exactly* what I had said, literally, and the reader had taken it metaphorically. "This early in the day John rarely stopped." "'Can I help you carry the bags?' John said eagerly, 'Can I? I'm big enough!' Williams smiled at him and shook his head. 'Not yet, John,' he said. 'A little bit later, maybe.'" "Williams was having trouble now keeping up with John's ever-lengthening stride." Later on, I counted on the reader not immediately picking up on discrepancies such as the little boy, John, being able to take over carrying the heavy bags, and I did my best to distract them from thinking about them until it was time to tip my hand.

This is another one of your stories which leans very heavily on misdirection. Very much like your earlier "Playing the Game." You work very hard on giving the reader the impression that they're seeing everything in an almost

cinematic way, while at the same time keeping their eyes averted from what is most important. They don't actually see the boy, except in little glimpses.

Gardner Dozois: That's a technique I've always liked. I don't think that it's a technique that goes over really well with most readers, though, who don't like you to be tricky. Which makes me wonder how the story ended up winning a Nebula in the first place.

I was going to ask you. Why do you think this story hit?

Gardner Dozois: I think it's because in spite of the fact that I was being tricky and using all those stage misdirections, there *is* a freight of honest emotion to the story. It ends with the final twist that the character you thought is the old man throughout the story is actually the *son* of the person who is afflicted by this time-shifting problem, who originally seemed to be *his* father. At the end of the story, after he gets his father, now grown into an ancient man again, to go to sleep, he breaks down and weeps. I think perhaps the fact that there was this emotionality or sentimentality to the story made up for the fact that it was an obscure and oblique bit of tricky stage misdirection.

It's also an astonishing compressed work. It's very short, and yet there's not only the human story in the foreground, but in the background there's this extraordinarily strange war going on, in which the weapons or entities involved are large and powerful and incomprehensible to the participants in the war.

Gardner Dozois: What I wanted to get across there, and which I think I managed to do, was indeed the fact that—much like Vernor Vinge's "singularity" idea—this war and this future had grown so incomprehensible that even the people who were *living* through it couldn't understand what was happening anymore. I deliberately kept it all at arm's length, something that was happening off over the valley hundreds of miles away or on the horizon, so that I wouldn't have to be too specific about *what* was happening. I wanted to convey an emotional feeling, one I've sometimes had myself sometimes while watching night howitzer barrages or night maneuvers, of vast incomprehensible forces moving in purposeful but to you incomprehensible ways. So I tried to keep everything off in the distance. I just describe strange noises and shapes and shadows. I mean, obviously they are doing *something*, and it's probably all very high-tech and logical if you knew enough about the science to understand what it is. But to these poor grunts caught in the middle, it is all just bewildering. They are veterans, participants in the wars, and even they don't understand what is going on in the war anymore. It's evolved to such a point of strangeness that even the veterans don't really understand what's happening anymore. Which is indeed a feeling that most veterans get in the middle of a war. Particularly a surreal, high tech war like the Vietnam War.

The two of them have come home through a war zone. Is this thematic, a searching for home, or have they come there simply because everything got so meaningless that one place is as good as another and home is just an arbitrary destination they head for?

Gardner Dozois: Both, I think. I think there is a feeling that they came out of even stranger and even more incomprehensibly bizarre territory further to the south, where the action is more intense. Basically things have grown so strange in the world that they're just looking for something familiar that they can put their foot down on. Some place where they can get a sense of normality. And, of course, the irony is that their home is changed beyond recognition when they reach it, just as they themselves are changed beyond recognition.

An interesting sidelight is that when I wrote the original three or four pages of the story, many many many years ago, I was living in Milford, Pennsylvania, and I wrote those pages in a notebook in longhand, sitting on the steps of Damon Knight's house, the Anchorage. Which I describe in a ruined condition in the opening pages of the story, although it was perfectly intact at the time. Years later, decades later, I went back to Milford and I visited the former site of the Anchorage—it had become ruined in the interval—and it was uncanny to see how closely I had described what it actually came to look like. The place did end up looking a lot like the description in the story, which I wrote while sitting on the steps of a perfectly intact house that didn't look anything like that at the time.

So that gave me a sort of a time-looping feeling.

I should probably add that I was proud of my idealism or whatever you want to call it, my naïvete, with this particular story in that before OMNI bought it, PLAYBOY offered to buy it and was going to pay me a very large amount of money. But the changes that they wanted in the story were changes that I couldn't live with. So I declined the offer and sold it to OMNI.

And in the way that the world inevitably rewards virtue, you therefore won the Nebula.

Gardner Dozois: That's probably true. I doubt that it would have won a Nebula if it had appeared in PLAYBOY. I'm surprised enough that it won a Nebula appearing in OMNI. Or anywhere else, for that matter. But I had just won a Nebula the year before, so I guess that sensitized the voters, as sometimes happens, to the idea of giving me another one. It was a brief Nebula-winning window that opened up for me and then closed again, slamming shut like the great doors of the grave.

"Few of the folk in Faerie would have anything to do with the computer salesman. He worked himself up and down one narrow, twisting street after another, until his feet throbbed and his arms ached from lugging the sample cases, and it seemed like days had passed rather than hours, and *still* he had not made a single sale. Barry Levingston considered himself a first-class salesman, one of the *best*, and he wasn't used to this kind of failure. It discouraged and frustrated him, and as the afternoon wore endlessly on—there was something funny about the way time passed here in Faerie; the hazy, bronze-colored Fairyland sun had hardly moved at all across the smoky amber sky since he'd arrived, although it should certainly be evening by *now*—he could feel himself beginning to lose that easy confidence and unshakable self-esteem that are the successful salesman's most essential stock-in-trade. He tried to tell himself that it wasn't really *his* fault. He was working under severe restrictions, after all. The product was new and unfamiliar to this particular market, and he was going "cold sell." There had been no telephone solicitation programs to develop leads, no ad campaigns, not so much as a demographic study of the market potential. Still, his total lack of success was depressing."

"Golden Apples of the Sun," which you co-wrote with Jack Dann and some hack or other, appeared in the March 1984 issue of PENTHOUSE. I've written my version of how this came about in your collection *Slow Dancing Through Time*. This time let's hear your version.

Gardner Dozois: As I recall, your take on the origin of the story in *Slow Dancing* is pretty much correct. At least, I think I agree more with your version than I agree with Jack's. As I recall, we were sitting around in my apartment. We had already done a couple of collaborations at that point, so we were actively looking for stories that we could collaborate on...

We called ourselves The Fiction Factory at that point. Although not in front of anybody who might write it down.

Gardner Dozois: Yes, imagine what John Clute would have said if he'd known we called ourselves The Fiction Factory! He would not have been pleased. He wasn't pleased as it was, as I recall. Unpleased with our felicity, I believe he was.

But we were sitting around in my living room in Quince Street, and Jack had been telling us about his experiences as a door-to-door salesman, doing cold sell for whatever product it was he was selling in those days.

Cable television.

Gardner Dozois: Cable television! That's right. He was in on the early days of cable television. He would go door-to-door convincing people to get cable television. He was talking about the difficulties of this, and the various kinds of customers you run into, and their different kinds of sales resistance. He said that we should write a story about this, using his experience, and his original idea was rather lame as I recall. Something about the Frankenstein monster going door-to-door.

Not entirely a bad image. But it didn't suggest a story.

Gardner Dozois: Somehow we got started talking about Fairyland at the same time. I believe you have an anecdote about this.

Don Keller and his then-wife Tatiana had been by, and Tatiana had said something you thought was very interesting and you were quoting her. Jack said, "Who's Tatiana?" You went on and mentioned her name again, and again he asked "Who's Tatiana?" You went on and mentioned her name again and he asked "Who's Tatiana?" a third time. So I said, "She's Don Keller's wife," You looked up and said, "She's also queen of the fairies."

Jack, in that very deadpan way of his said, "Jeeze, that's kind of a comedown, isn't it? 'I used to be queen of the fairies and now I'm Don Keller's wife!'"

Then you started playing with the idea and had the queen of the fairies selling computers in Perth Amboy.

Gardner Dozois: So this totally random remark got us talking about Fairyland, and in the context of our previous conversation about selling door-to-door, the idea occurred to *somebody,* might have been me, might have been Jack, I really don't remember, that we could have a salesman working door-to-door in the world of Faerie. To emphasize the incongruity between the fantastic setting and the mundane aspect of the task.

It might have been you who suggested that selling computers to them would increase the contrast even further. As I recall it, I think that once again it was Jack who sat down and actually wrote the first few pages, though they were later reworked by you and then reworked again by me. But it was Jack who wrote the opening few pages, where he's knocking on doors and fairies are coming out and reacting to him in different ways

One of the engines that made these collaborations actually work was that Jack, with vast energy and enthusiasm, would actually *write* some copy on these ideas, and then, faced with this, the rest of us would have to *react* to the fact that there was this stack of copy sitting there, and work on it ourselves.

Jack would sit down and write the section that nobody else

wanted to write. I had no interest whatsoever in writing about a salesman plodding door-to-door. But faced with an already written section, I was perfectly happy to *rewrite* it.

Gardner Dozois: Of course, he was the one who'd had the actual experience of being a door-to-door salesman. So he was the logical person to write about it. Neither of us had had any experience with that sort of thing.

Jack, of course, would react with great enthusiasm, as if writing this section were the most wonderful thing he could possibly do.

Gardner Dozois: This is why a lot of these collaborations happened. Jack would sit down and write some copy. I have a feeling that, being fundamentally lazy, if it had been left to me, I would have thought about it for a couple of days and said, "Nyah, that's a really stupid idea," and not bothered to have actually *produced* any copy about it. So most of these collaborations probably would never have come to fruition, except for the fact that the great pulsing engine of Jack Dann was there, churning out page after page. After he'd ripped out ten pages, we would then become embarrassed that he had put all this *effort* into it, and decide that we actually had to complete the story after all.

I believe this went around the circle a couple of times. I remember what I liked best about the story were the descriptive parts you had written with this bronze-skied, weirdly evocative Faerie. They reminded me of some of the better fairy pictures done by Victorian lunatics.

Gardner Dozois: I don't recall that Jack had a lot to do with the rest of the story, after he wrote the initial sequence, which takes up the first seven or eight pages of the story. I think mostly the rest of it was hammered out between you and me. It was pretty much complete as to plot when I did my final polishing draft on it.

What I wanted to do in that final draft was put in stuff like the stuff you were just describing. It was too jokey and not evocative enough, and even in an UNKNOWN WORLDS type story, I thought that a story that took place in the land of Faerie ought to also have flashes of wonder and strangeness and lyricism in it as well as the jokes about the computer salesman having his ass turned into grass and so forth. I tried to work those touches in over the existing plot. Which I thought was fairly successful.

I also tried to burnish up the mythological richness of the fairy stuff. I spent a week or so looking through books of mythology and I worked in obscure references to various mythological tropes, having them swear by invoking Celtic deities and so forth. And work that all into the background. Not really affecting the direction or plot of the story much, but just sort of burnishing the surface and giving it a deeper texture.

Whose idea was the leftist troll?

Gardner Dozois: I'm pretty sure the *troll* himself was yours. Morrig the Fearsome was entirely your idea. You showed up one day and you had written the Morrig the Fearsome section. Now, the idea of having him speak like an old Trotskyite or Wobbly or union organizer was mine, and I reworked your section to reflect that. But the whole basic idea of what happened in that section was yours.

So *why* did I want him to speak like an old Wobbly union organizer? I don't have the slightest idea. Except, again, that it was incongruous. It's probably something that survived from memory of reading an old L. Sprague de Camp and Fletcher Pratt story when I was a kid.

On the other hand, I believe that the twist, ultimate ending where Faerie begins to invade the computer systems of Earth was your idea. I think you had added that twist. I don't think that was my contribution.

As I recall, the story kind of lurched forward in plot. We never had a definite end in mind. Whatever was handed over to the other person, it was obvious what part of the story came next, so we wrote it on the fly.

Gardner Dozois: It clearly needed a twist of some kind. That's one of the twists we could have used, and that seemed perfectly adequate, so we used it. I suppose any number of other twist ending could have been come up with. But it did need some kind of twist or kicker at the end.

I was the one who came up with the title, incidentally. I brought my first draft to you entitled "Golden APPLES of the Sun." With the word apples all in caps.

Gardner Dozois: I am perfectly willing to give total credit for the appalling pun concealed in the title to you.

And then you guys started jumping up and down about what a wonderful title it was. But it was never meant to be the title. It was just a joke.

Gardner Dozois: Well, in fact, when I sent the manuscript in to PENTHOUSE, I received a call from someone there, an assistant editor, who told me that we couldn't call the story "Golden Apples of the Sun" because that was "a line from a Ray Bradbury story." Apparently he had never heard of Yeats. But not wanting to infringe on Ray Bradbury's territory, they therefore summarily changed the title to "Virgin Territory." Which I thought was a horrible title, and quickly turned the title back as soon as we reprinted it in *Slow Dancing*.

I wonder if you would have come up with that title a few years later? You don't hear that much about Apples anymore. This was right at the beginning of the home computer revolution, when all that anybody really knew about was Apples. I suspect that if we'd written this story a few years later, you would not have come up with that particular joke.

We should say a word about the editing. This was a twelve thousand word story, and they asked us to cut six thousand words. Which is literally in half. You and I got together over the course of a long and bloody afternoon and took our knives to it. And since I liked the story marginally less than you did, I outlasted you. We got it down to six thousand five hundred, and were knee deep in adjectives and viscera, and you had lost the will to live. You just sat there with your head down, mumbling, "I don't know, I don't know, maybe I should just kill myself."

Gardner Dozois: Unlike "Morning Child," where I had gone into this fit of noble-mindedness and turned down PLAYBOY's offer of big bucks because I didn't want to make the changes they wanted in the story, I think that at some point with this story I decided, "Oh, fuck it. I just want the money." I was willing to go along with these changes, probably because I didn't take the story as seriously *as* a story as I took "Morning Child."

When we reprinted the story in *Slow Dancing in Time*, I did go over both drafts, and incorporated them, and tried to be fair to the idea that it ought to be cut. And indeed some of the original version probably *should* have been cut. There were some valid cuts that I let stand. But in the end, I ended up putting it back a lot closer to what we had had in mind in the first place. Since we really had been cutting out everything we could possibly cut out towards the end of the marathon editing section.

We went through it first and cut out a scene or two that were just comic, extraneous. We went through it again, and cut out paragraphs. Then sentences. Then we went through it again looking for adjectives and adverbs that could be cut without changing the meaning. Then we went through it again and changed all the "did nots" to "didn'ts." Until we got it down to 5,999 words. In retrospect, they probably would've let us get away with 6,200.

Gardner Dozois: Better safe than sorry, I guess. I haven't looked at the cut version in years. I'm not even sure I still have a copy of it. But I suspect that, although it may be slightly overwritten, perhaps, in places, I prefer the longer, fuller version of the story.

What has always boggled me is that PENTHOUSE felt that their readers would be *interested* in this story in the first place. If they were intending, by changing the name of the story to "Virgin Territory," to give a wink-wink hint of salaciousness, to imply that this story was going to be hot stuff, then their readers must have been very disappointed and puzzled, because there is practically not a whiff of sex in the story. There is one distant view of sex, galloping by in the background, but that's as close as it gets. So the typical PENTHOUSE reader looking for a good story to whack off to in the john must've been puzzled and disappointed when they hit this particular story.

"The wizard sat alone at a table in Schrafft's, eating a tuna sandwich on rye. He finished off the last bite of his sandwich, sat back, and licked a spot of mayonnaise off his thumb. There was an ozone crackle in the air, and his familiar, a large brindle cat, materialized in the chair opposite him."

"Afternoon at Schrafft's," with Jack Dann and yours truly, appeared in AMAZING STORIES, March 1984, edited by George Scithers. We started this at my house...

Gardner Dozois: "Afternoon at Schrafft's" was totally *your* fault. I certainly never would have written this story if left to myself. But I was badgered into it by you and Jack. We were over at your house and you had cannily gotten us all drunk, and we were sitting around and you said "We should do another collaboration." And you started throwing out ideas. I was well aware that we were all too drunk to really come up with anything worthwhile. But you insisted we had to start writing a story *right then.*

Nobody could really think of anything to write a story about. It had come up earlier in the evening that Jack and I were doing one anthology that featured cats, one anthology that featured dinosaurs (though that dinosaur book did not sell for years), and an anthology that featured wizards. So either you or Jack, I think it was you, came up with the canny idea that we should come up with a story that featured a cat, a dinosaur, and a wizard, so we could reprint it in all three anthologies. When push came to shove, we only reprinted it in one anthology. I don't even remember which. I think it was the cat anthology. Do you remember?

It was *Magicats*.

Gardner Dozois: But we didn't reprint it in the other two, so it was sort of a waste of time. Jack, of course, immediately caught fire with enthusiasm...

You could talk him into anything. "Here, Jack, eat this frog. It'll be great!"

Gardner Dozois: Jack immediately took the bit in his teeth and began rushing ahead, describing an opening for this story. I'm almost positive he's the one who threw Schrafft's into the mix.

He said he'd always wanted to write a story set in Schrafft's Restaurant.

Gardner Dozois: Yes, I've never even *been* to Schrafft's Restaurant.

It turned out neither had he. He had no idea what it looked like. When it came time for him to describe the restaurant, he decided it must look pretty much like any other restaurant.

Gardner Dozois: Jack had the obsession with Schrafft's. I'm not sure I had even *heard* of Schrafft's before that. But you and he werc going full speed, plotting the story, and I was drunk enough that, against my better judgment, I began to participate in this.

Actually, you got into it because you couldn't resist pointing out the things we were getting wrong. We'd say something and you'd say, "No, no, no, that's not how you do it." It was the editor in you begging to be let out.

Gardner Dozois: I certainly hope younger generations, when they read this, will find it appalling how these monuments to art actually come into being. I don't know that there is really much to say about the story. Once we decided there had to be a cat and a dinosaur and a wizard in it, and once Jack had imposed the fiat that it had to take place in Schrafft's, I'm not sure how much else we could actually have done with the story, other than what we did with it.

I'm trying to remember who actually wrote the opening.

I did. I took the notes and placed them on my desk and went back to work on my usual stuff. Then, a couple of days later I didn't feel like working on whatever I was working on, so I picked this up and in my free time, to treat myself, wrote up the first draft of those parts who had been described. It went to Jack after that, which was when we discovered he didn't know what Schrafft's looked like. And then to you.

Gardner Dozois: Jack put in all the cabalistic stuff. Which is still incomprehensible to me. I have no idea if he got it correct or not. In fact, I'm not sure if *he* knows if he got it correct or not.

I'm sure he put in a lot of research. Only Jack would do a lot of research into a light little joke story, to make sure the Cabala is correct.

Gardner Dozois: When the wizard does his spell, he invokes all of this cabalistic lore. That was all Jack, I'm sure. I remember trying to make the story funnier when it got to my draft. Indeed, most of the comic Yiddish dialogue was put in by me. As it has been put in by me in almost all of our collaborations with Jack. Everybody says, "Oh, Jack, wrote all the comic Yiddish shtick dialog," when usually Jack *didn't* write the comic Yiddish shtick dialog. So what can I tell you? So, *nu?*

I just tried to make it funnier. At some point we needed the wizard to accidentally turn himself into a dinosaur. Because we insisted there had to be a dinosaur in there. There was no particular other reason. I went and picked the brains of Bob Walters, our local dinosaur expert, for some reasonable dinosaur to turn into, and what it would have looked like and what the name of it was. That was where we got the dinosaur from.

It's a totally innocuous little piece of fluff. I think it's a pleasant read.

At one point, Jack and I did up a children's book version of it. Some editor had actually asked us for a children's book. We worked up a version of "Afternoon at Schrafft's." It got sent around to a couple of places, but nobody was interested in it. I think it's a charming little story in its own way. It certainly doesn't have a brain in its head. There's not a profound bone in its entire body. But it's got some decent jokes in it. The cat and the wizard have an interestingly amicable bickering relationship, which I think is amusing.

The only thing that comes close to a technical innovation is that when I got to the end of the story, I came up with three different last lines for the story. I'm very hipped to the importance of the last line and will often agonize over the importance of the last line for days. I came up with three different last lines I could use to end the story, and couldn't decide which to use. So I end-ed up using all three of them in sequence. Which is a technique I had used once before, in an obscure story called "The Storm." It seemed to work well enough there, so I used it here too.

I like to think that this is the kind of story that Thurber—on a really bad day, when he was drunk and had the flu—might have turned out. It has a sort of Thurberesque quality to it. I've always liked Thurber; I'm not sure if Jack does. *Jack's* parts have more of an Isaac Bashevis Singer quality. So it's as if Thurber and Isaac Bashevis Singer got *really* drunk in a hotel where they were having an illicit tryst one weekend and decided to write a story—the result would be sort of like "Afternoon at Schrafft's." They probably wouldn't have put a dinosaur in it, though.

Since we pretended that we were doing this for the money, I'd like to throw in the final outcome. Some time later, my agent sent me a check for two items. One was my third of the sale of "Golden Apples of the Sun" to PENTHOUSE, and the other was my third of the reprint of "Afternoon at Schrafft's" to your anthology. My share of which was nine

dollars, and you guys had out of the goodness of your hearts thrown in an extra dollar to pay for my agent's ten percent. So I stood holding this check for one thousand and nine dollars. I said to Marianne, "This is a funny business."

Gardner Dozois: Well, you wanted to be a writer. Kids, don't try this at home!

"It had been cold all that afternoon. When they picked Hassmann up at the gate that evening, it was worse than cold—it was freezing."

Next comes "Dinner Party," which first appeared in *Light Years and Dark*, an original anthology edited by Michael Bishop. I went back and reread this, and I'd remembered it being quite a short story, but it's not at all. It's a long short story.

Gardner Dozois: It just *seems* longer than it is. We call that the boredom factor.

I notice that it's deliberately designed to read slow. It has very long paragraphs. It has a stately pace. You were trying to build up the tension, I think, by making the reader wait for the payoff.

Gardner Dozois: I've always had long paragraphs. I'm not sure how consciously crafted this is. In fact, I used to have *really* long paragraphs. There are several of my early stories where a paragraph could stretch for two or three pages. Eventually someone hammered into my head that this was not a very good idea, so I began breaking the paragraphs a little more frequently. But my paragraphs still tend to be longer than the average. Particularly in these days of journalistic, Hemingway-like prose, I'm very long-winded and I get into these descriptions of trees going by and stuff and other shit that nobody cares about particularly. But that's the way it comes out.

Actually, I think it works quite well. It's an exquisitely-crafted story. Particularly since you've set yourself a very difficult task here. Which is that you don't tell the reader what's going on until the very end of the story. And so you have to keep the reader's interest through the bulk of it, just by making him or her wonder what's going on.

Gardner Dozois: I thought it would be more effective that way, if they didn't really understand what was going on until the end of the story. Obviously they know there's *something* portentous going on. I think one of the ways the story keeps the reader on the page is wondering just why they're taking this kid off under these unusual circumstances and what in the world is going to happen to him. That was one of the devices I used to keep the reader with the story until the end.

Right in the middle of the story, there's a short episode where the young soldier's in the Cadillac with the politician and the politician's reticent wife, and they hit a patch of ice. For a second the Cadillac goes out of control, and the politician is behind the wheel wildly trying to regain control. And there's a flash of fear and anger on his face. It struck me that that one image neatly encapsulates everything that was going on in the story. It's like a glimpse of the truth behind the civil mask that everyone's wearing.

Gardner Dozois: That was the intention. It shows what the politician is trying to suppress or not admit to. The politician is playing this on the surface very much like this is a normal social occasion. Of course the soldier is not buying into this, but he's cooperating with the politician in erecting this social facade. They're all working with the social facade to some degree, all three of the characters. The wife to the least. She plays as little as her husband will let her get away with. But the politician is relentlessly forcing this pretense of normality on the situation. Because he's powerless, essentially, the soldier's going along with this as well as he can. But the politician's losing control of the car is an indication of what the politician is feeling underneath.

I think the soldier is almost glad to see that, in a way. It's more of the truth than the hypocritical play that they're living out in going out on this dinner date.

There's a revolution or a civil war brewing in the background, which hasn't quite arrived. But you don't establish any particular grievances the people have against the government. You just wanted to have a rebellion to act as a motive force for the events.

Gardner Dozois: I didn't really pin down the specifics. I see it as a kind of a libertarian/states' rights kind of an issue, where states struggle to break away from Federal control. Which is something that crops up from time to time, particularly in the West, even to this day. I wrote this story before anybody knew much about militia groups in Montana and so forth. So that was still pretty much subliminal in society at that point. But you could see the little signs here and there that there are many people who would like to fragment the Union and to have all the states running themselves and not having a Federal government and so forth. I sort of hint in that direction by having the graffiti "FUCK THE UNION" on the wall at one point.

It's sort of a general Balkanization collapse process that is underway here, much as we *later* saw in what they now call "the former Yugoslavia." Where, as soon as the controlling Federal authority is gone, everything flies apart and old hatreds re-emerge and everybody's goes at each other's throats.

I found myself feeling a fair amount of sympathy for this crusty old bastard of a politician, who is, after all, trying to hold things together.

Gardner Dozois: That's interesting, because I think that's there to some extent. The politician is *personally* dislikeable—I don't think that I would like him, if we were to meet socially. But in a way he is working for the good side, as far as you can identify the good side in a situation like this, in that he's trying to hold our civilization and our society as we know it together. And he's willing to pay almost any price to do this.

In a way, the soldier, who's much more likeable, represents the tendency to want our society to fly apart. And the indication to me that it probably is *going* to fly apart, in terms of the story, is the fact that he comes to the particular self-realization that he does at the end. He doesn't *want* civilization to hang together. In fact, he's looking forward to it all flying apart and everybody knifing and shooting each other in the alleys.

It's a situation where the most dislikeable character is standing in for the forces of law and order and civilization, which adds a little frisson to the story, I think.

When they arrived at the restaurant and opened the doors and were mobbed by reporters, that came as a complete surprise. It made sense in the story, but I certainly was not expecting that when it happened.

Gardner Dozois: Whether the reporters were called by the politician or not is something I never actually pin down. It's not impossible that he would have alerted them himself, to milk the maximum amount of PR value from the situation.

I think it comes as a surprise because the rest of the story is so isolated. I mean, it's the gate guard and the soldier huddling by themselves in the middle of the night, and there's nobody around. A lone car comes up. There's nobody else around. He goes and gets in the car, and there's the interaction with the people in the car. But you're set up to anticipate a situation where there's only a few people around, and then suddenly you get a crowd of people—that's probably why it surprises you.

Finally, you explain what's happening, and then there's the snapper at the very end. But what you do is have the soldier say, "No, sir," and then you describe the reaction that's going to happen after he delivers his final words, in rather a lot of detail, and *then* he delivers the words.

Gardner Dozois: Well, yeah, I did that deliberately, because I wanted the story to funnel down to the soldier's final words, and there wasn't any good way to have him say them and *then* work in the reactions of the politician and other people without diluting the effect of the final words. So, as you say, I worked the reactions in in advance, in anticipation of what was going to happen. I did want to end with those final words as the last words of the story, and it seemed to me that it wouldn't be as effective to have the reaction shots afterwards. So I had my reaction shots in advance.

Any last thoughts about this story?

Gardner Dozois: I should probably mention that the inspiration for this particular story goes all the way back to the Sixties, when I was reading a newspaper that came out shortly after the Kent State massacre—I forget which paper it was; it might have been a New York Paper, it might have been a Philly paper, I don't remember. But anyway, in one of these papers there was a letter to the editor from somebody in support of the action that the National Guardsmen had taken at Kent State, saying that you had to hold society together from the forces of chaos that wanted to fragment it, no matter *what* the price was. The letter writer went on to say that even if his own son was one of the people who was shot by National Guardsman in some campus unrest in the future, he would go up and shake the Guardsman's hand, and congratulate him on doing his duty, however hard it had been, and that he would even *take him out and buy him dinner* to show him that he appreciated the role that he was playing in holding society together.

This stuck in my head, and sat there for a number of years. The idea that somebody would *call* him on it, and he'd actually have to take his son's killer out to dinner. Then, when I finally did get around writing this story, it was too late to make it a Kent State story. That was all in the past and anyway it would not have been science fiction, so I probably would not have been able to sell it. So I started to think, well, what about a Kent State-like situation in the future? Which is where I came up with this background of the Balkanization of the United States. Of course there's all sorts of issues in the background, probably, that the story doesn't get into.

But just that idea of that guy who had written that letter to the editor being made to eat his words...being made to actually *take* the guy who shot and killed his son out to dinner, was really the basic nub of the whole story. The irony here is that the politician is taking him out to dinner to show that the role of the soldier in killing the boy was to hold society together and keep our civilization going and all of that, and of course the self-revelation that the soldier has is that he *didn't* really do it because of all of those reasons. It was *fun* to shoot people and kill them.

Of course, that's too simple. He did it because he was told to do it. But he's not reacting to it the way that he's supposed to be reacting to it, or the way that the politician would *like* him to react to it, that it was a painful necessity, a duty, something that he had to do. He's reacting to it as though, "Well, yeah, I was told to do it, and I had to do it, but, you know, it was kind of fun. I kind of liked it."

The soldier himself is not real happy with this revelation. But he's in the end forced to confront it and deal with it. I think it's a good indication that this society is in for a lot of trouble, because even those who're supposed to be holding the civilization together, actually, in their heart of hearts, want it to fly apart and dissolve in chaos and blood and old night. So that's a pretty good indication that they're not going to be able to hold this particular Humpty Dumpty together.

I might add that I was unable to sell this only mildly politically controversial story anywhere in the genre at the time. It was too "dangerous" for all the SF magazine markets of the early '80s, a particularly timid and narrow period in the history of the magazine market. If it hadn't been for the fact that Michael Bishop was putting an anthology together at that point and asked me to send him a story, it might never have seen print at all.

"The cops started to file into the stadium at the bottom of the ninth inning, and the crowd buzzed like a huge angry bee, an ominous razor-edged hum that set your teeth on edge."

I'm going to skip over "The Mayan Variation" until next time, because I've misplaced my copy of it, and it's not collected.

Gardner Dozois: It's not all that much of a story anyway. It's just basically a joke story.

Well, maybe we can take a whack at it anyway, then. Let's see. It appeared in the September, 1984, issue of AMAZING, edited by George Scithers. So let's start with a brief synopsis of the plot.

Gardner Dozois: The plot is that they play this baseball game, and...I guess it's similar, in a way, to the trick that I use in "Dinner Party." They play this baseball game, and there's obviously a *lot* riding on it. The stakes are higher than usual, even, in a ball game, and everybody's very tense. They play the ball game, and then at the end it turns out that they've instituted this custom where the losing team is taken and executed on the playing field with much ceremony right after the game. This is considered to be a great honor, of course.

This totally trivial story came from me reading something about the Mayan sport which was a ball game of sorts (more similar to soccer, actually, or basketball, than to baseball), and where the losing team would be executed at the end of the game, sacrificed to the gods. A great honor, they got to go right to Heaven. That was in my mind. This was at a period where Susan was watching a lot of baseball games, so I was sitting through baseball games every night, and so these things came together in my head and I decided to write a baseball story. Almost certainly the only baseball story I will ever write.

That was a time when I was doing a lot of things I never had done before in my career and probably never will do again. I guess out of an excess of energy. I wrote a baseball story, I wrote a bar story. Neither of these are forms that I work with a lot.

So I guess the question is, in retrospect, admitting that these are minor stories, and the money is all spent now, are you sorry that you wrote them or glad?

Gardner Dozois: No, I'm not sorry that I wrote them. I mean, they are what they are. I think "The Mayan Variation" is an entertaining little story. I think that most readers of that particular issue of the magazine probably didn't feel like they had been cheated out of their money. They probably felt that they got their money's worth out of reading it.

It's hardly a milestone in modern literature, or even in science fiction. But having written it, no, I don't regret that I wrote it. Would I write it again, now, if I hadn't written it in the first place? Probably not. But what's done is done. You can't disown your children, even the gimpy ones with web toes and too many fingers and eyes.

———

"They were outside, unlashing the Mars lander, when the storm blew up."

———

The next story, "The Gods of Mars" appeared in OMNI, March 1985. Ellen Datlow was the editor, and it was co-written with Jack Dann and some guy who used to be a writer but now ekes out a miserable existence doing interviews.

Gardner Dozois: Yes, and you were so promising, too! If you hadn't decided to waste your life doing this academic interviewing crap, you probably could've won a Hugo someday.

How did we get started on this story? That was the Fiction Factory, right? Just sitting around, talking.

Gardner Dozois: As I recall, we were consciously looking for a story to write. I told the story of its origin in *Slow Dancing Through Time*. I believe that was fundamentally true. I was looking through one of my old story idea notebooks, and for some time in there I had had a note about the first Mariner flight to Mars, and how, as it came into orbit, but before it could take any photos, a huge sandstorm came up, and by the time the sandstorm died and they actually *got* pictures of the Martian surface, they were all surprised to see that it didn't look anything like what they had *expected* it to look like. It occurred to me that maybe it actually *had* been the way that they were expecting to see it, but that the sandstorm had been quickly whipped up and under the cover of this, some preternatural agency had rearranged everything. So that when the sandstorm died, we saw *not* the surface that everyone had expected to see, the Burroughs Mars, with canals, but rather the surface that showed up in the Mariner photographs.

I jotted this note down in my notebook. Many years went by, and this was one of many ideas I threw out at that particular brainstorming session. I think we were sitting around what I used to laughingly call my back yard, which was a square of concrete with a fence around it at the rear of my Quince Street apartment. I think it was in the summer. This was one of the story possibilities that I threw out. Why you guys particularly reacted to *that* one and decided to go with it, I don't remember at this remove.

I do remember, however, that we decided that it called for a high-tech hard science opening with a space crew in orbit around Mars. And since Jack and I had never written much with space ships in it, we decided that this was *your* job. So we turned it over to you, to write the high-tech hard science spaceship opener. Which you did.

In fact, when I wrote that scene, I had somebody deploying some hardware using a spanner, which I figured was the most ANALOG-type tool you could possibly have. I should say on our behalf that the reason we were always looking for stories was that when we came up with one, they were

like found money. They were all works we wouldn't have written otherwise, that got us attention, and earned money, and were actually quite popular.

Gardner Dozois: Neither Jack nor I would have written that story by ourselves, because...Well, I can't speak for Jack. Jack has showed himself in the past willing to tackle just about any project, no matter how daunting or formidable. So *he* might have bluffed his way through it. *I* never would've written that story, because I wouldn't have felt capable of writing the high-tech hard science NASA-in-orbit section. Whereas *you* probably wouldn't have thought of the Barsoom-coming-back-into-existence part of the idea, because you were not an Edgar Rice Burroughs fan.

I went and read five or six of the Barsoom novels as research, in order to find all this bright, detailed, Edgar Rice Burroughs-ish color, and discovered that there *was* no color. He mentions that there are canals, and low, lichen-covered hills which John Carter runs over a lot. Every now and then he comes to a fortress or a city, and there's a fight. And that's all.

Gardner Dozois: *Ocher* hills! They're always *ocher* hills.

That's right. There was quite a striking paucity of invention in those books. It was disillusioning.

Gardner Dozois: And yet *somehow* these books have left me with a store of wonderful images in my head. I think that you read them too late in life. There's a window of opportunity for reading Edgar Rice Burroughs. It opens up when you're about twelve, and have no critical faculties whatsoever.

If you read him at this age, you can sort of filter out all the crap, like a baleen whale, and you're left with a store of evocative images. But if you wait until you develop any critical faculties, it's too late. The writing gets in the way.

You had a plot line where the protagonist was a black astronaut trying to live up to his father's high expectations, which he'd never managed to do.

Gardner Dozois: Actually, one or the other of *you* came up with the fact that one of the astronauts was black. Being faced with this as a given, I thought that he needed to have more psychological depth, since he was the character upon whom the plot was going to pivot. So on one of my rewrites, I worked on giving him more background and complexity as a character, rather than just being one of the astronauts who's just labeled as being black. His frustrations and things he needed to work through needed to be brought more closely to the surface.

It's true that simply being African-American is not much in the way of characterization.

Gardner Dozois: "Hi, I'm black!" Whether I would have made him black in the first place, I don't know. But having been given that as a given by one or the other of you, it seemed like that needed to made more of a factor, psychologically, in the story line. So I worked in some of that stuff about his relationship with his father, and so forth.

It also gave me the chance to work in a mention of an old Ron Cobb cartoon which I'd always liked. Which showed a black astronaut sweeping up around the camp site of Apollo 43 or something. That seemed to sum up my take on how NASA felt about the whole thing.

A lot of those details are true. I did end up doing some research into this stuff. Into NASA and so forth. They really do—or did, at least; I don't know if they still bother—spy on the crews. During the Skylab and early space shots, they really did tape and listen to everything that was said in the space ship or the space lab. They had psychologists poring over it, and it really could affect your subsequent career if you were spotted saying something unwholesome or Un-American. The astronauts knew that. If you read *A House in Space*, they knew that they were under observation twenty-four hours a day.

The ending we were quite shameless with. We actually gave them the old Bambi-is-dead riff. They all crack their helmets, believing that they're all going to live in this Edgar Rice Burroughs Mars, and they all die. And the commander back on the orbiter mourns them and braces himself for the long, lonely trip home. After which we reveal that in some alternative sense they didn't really die at all.

Gardner Dozois: That's the whole point of the story. That from the perspective of one universe, they've died; and from the perspective of another universe, they *haven't* died; and there's almost no connection between those two universes. It's like Schrödinger's Cat. In one universe, the wave function has collapsed so that they're alive and they're walking around, swimming in the canals. In another universe the wave function has collapsed so that they're all lying there dead on the rusty, airless soil. It depends on which reality you've collapsed into, what the outcome is.

That was sort of the whole point of the story, that you choose your own universe. They are offered the opportunity to choose between the Mars of the Mariner probes and a generalized Edgar Rice Burroughs-like Mars, even though we don't use any of his specific tropes. A living Mars, at any rate. Each one of them decides which reality they're going to inhabit.

As I recall, after we got through the high-tech opening, with the space crew in orbit around Mars, we decided to turn things over to our phenomenology expert, who was Jack.

Jack injected a lot of the phenomenology into it, in fact. I seemed to recall that we took a partial draft of the story up to Jack during the weekend that he was getting *married*, in Binghamton.

God, we were shameless.

Gardner Dozois: We gave it to him, and he worked on it for a while. Then it came back, I think, to you. And then I did a unifying draft on it. Mostly, as I said, beefing up the characterization of the viewpoint character.

I think we also rewrote the ending two or three times, trying to get it to work better. It may be that in the first draft—although I don't really have a clear memory of this—that they are just shown walking off into the living Martian landscape. I wanted there to be more of this either-or wave-function-collapsing duality. So I believe that we added the scene where, from the point of view of the Commander, they're all dead. And then went back for the coda in which, from their point of view, in *their* reality, they're all alive and jumping around and swimming in the canal. At any rate, we worked on the ending a bit.

This was later published in OMNI, And was a Nebula finalist. Which made "Sue Denim" very unhappy in CHEAP TRUTH.

Lew Shiner spit nails.

Gardner Dozois: He basically said we were polluting SF's precious bodily fluids.

"The C. Fred Johnson Municipal Pool was packed with swimmers, more in spite of the blazing sun and wet, muggy heat than because of them."

"The Clowns," co-written with Susan Casper and Jack Dann, appeared in PLAYBOY in August 1985, and...

Gardner Dozois: ...and ever since Susan's been telling people that a picture of her appeared in PLAYBOY.

Susan Casper: Yeah, I had my picture in PLAYBOY. It's fun to tell people that.

Gardner Dozois: They're all very impressed.

Susan Casper: They are!

Gardner Dozois: Some young girl last night in the Internet chat said, "Wow! You must have been pretty!"

Susan Casper: Well, I was. I still *am*.

The other stories you two were doing in collaboration at the same time were humorous, and this one is anything but humorous. How did this get started?

Susan Casper: Gardner had this idea he'd been keeping in the back of his head for a very long time. He made the mistake of telling Jack about it...

Gardner Dozois: This was in 1983, November according to my notes. Jack and Susan and I were all sitting around in our old apartment on Quince Street. We were talking about weird stuff. We were having one of those conversations where you talk about freaky, weird, possibly supernatural things that you've seen or heard of.

Susan Casper: And you and Gardner and Jack had been doing an *awful* lot of collaborations, and Jack turned around to me—

I had not yet, at this point, had anything published—and told me that we really ought to do something together, because I had been writing for a while. I said yes, that sounded like a good idea to me, and he came up with this idea that Gardner had actually mentioned a long time ago. This was an idea for Jack and *I* to write, the two of us.

Gardner Dozois: No, earlier you and Jack were talking about how you ought to do a story together—then we had the conversation about weird stuff, and in the spirit of this conversation I related an anecdote that a guy had told to me in the Village. Years ago, when I used to live in the Village, I had known this guy who was a heavy drug user. The last time I had ever seen him, he told me about how clowns were following him around everywhere. Nobody else could see them but him. Part of the anecdote, which didn't get into the story, is that he would be alone in the apartment late at night, and he would get up and go into the bathroom, and there would be a clown sitting on the toilet, grinning at him. He would be riding on his motorcycle and he would feel cold arms close around his waist, and he would look over his shoulder and there'd be a clown riding behind him, grinning at him.

So I told this story, and as was his wont, Jack said, "Wow! What a great idea for a story! Susan, *that* can be the story that you and I write together!" You started talking about this story, and the next thing I knew, Jack had rushed over to the typewriter, and you were writing this story about invisible clowns.

Susan Casper: We'd gotten all of about four sentences.

Gardner Dozois: I was kind of sulky about this, because I had been carrying around this story idea for years, and now *you* were writing this story, and you weren't even consulting me or cutting me in on it! You talked about this story for the rest of the evening. The next day you were still working on the story,

and I finally got pissed and said, "Well, if you're going to write my story, then I have to be cut in on it!"
So I insisted on dealing myself into the collaboration.

Susan Casper: It was an interesting thing, though, at this point to be collaborating with the two of them because, as I said, I hadn't actually had anything published. Jack would send me manuscript—not much, a couple of lines—and an outline of where I should take it. I was sitting there going, this doesn't feel right, this doesn't sound right, and this dialog doesn't work right. But at the same time, being the unpublished member of the group, I felt kind of funny overwriting Jack, and saying, "No, it should go this way, and, no, the dialogue should sound like this, and, no, this is what they should say." But finally they convinced me that the only way it was going to work was if I just *did* it, the way I felt I ought to do it, and so that's what I eventually did.

I did a lot of the original writing on that story, and then I'd send it to Jack and he'd do a little bit, and then he'd send it back to me and I'd do more. Now what happened was while I did a lot of the original writing on the story, they both came along and overwrote what I wrote. So I don't feel like I did most of the story. But I certainly did most of the first draft.

Gardner Dozois: You had a good feel for the dialogue of the kid and his family. Your kid-and-family dialogue was actually more authentic-sounding than Jack's was. So you overwrote most of that, as I recall.

You made some basic changes in the original vision. The clowns are dressed in black and white, which was a sinister touch, and they're going around actively killing people, shoving them in front of cars and whatnot.

Susan Casper: It's funny, within a year it became a major motion picture. For which we never saw a *dime,* I might add.

Gardner Dozois: What was it called—*Clowns from Outer
Space?*

Susan Casper: Something like that. *Killer Clowns from Outer
Space,* I forget.

**That would have been a coincidence, right? Rather than
somebody actually stealing the idea?**

Gardner Dozois: Who knows? It *did* appear in PLAYBOY.

Susan Casper: It certainly was in a source where people could
have seen it.

Gardner Dozois: We didn't think it was actionable enough to
try to sue anybody over.

Susan Casper: Actually, we didn't find out about it until it was
too late.

Gardner Dozois: Of course, there *are* precedents for this. One
horror writer, I forget who it was, it might have been Robert
Bloch, was talking about what horror was. Horror was...

Susan Casper: You go to the circus, and you have fun, and you
buy a balloon, and you watch the clowns, and you laugh at the
clowns, and you have a wonderful time. And then you come
home from the circus, and you go into your apartment, you
open the closet and there's the clown.

Gardner Dozois: A lot of the stuff from the original anecdote
that the guy told me did not make it into the story. Because we
made it a child protagonist, he's not riding the motorcycle and
feeling the clown putting its arms around him. The going into
the bathroom and finding the clown there scene didn't make it
in either.

Susan Casper: We came up with the swimming pool sequence instead. Which actually works better, with the two children.

Gardner Dozois: Susan wrote perhaps the bulk of the story. What my contribution mostly was was working on the pacing. I tried to give it more of a suspense movie kind of pacing. I remember reworking several of these scenes to stretch them out in a way that would heighten tension.

Susan Casper: He also, as he always did with collaborations, went over and smoothed things out, because my prose and Jack's are nothing alike at all. You could see real obvious welds where the story had gone back and forth between the two of us, and where it left huge chunks of what Jack did, and pieces I'd rewritten, and stuff. He smoothed that out. I certainly was not capable of that at that point. I don't know if I'd be capable of that now.

You never do provide a rationale for who these clowns are, or why they're doing what they're doing.

Susan Casper: That's the point.

Gardner Dozois: There's a rationale, of course. As in *most* of my stories, you could read it that none of these events are really happening, and the kid is just insane. Or has gone insane.

Susan Casper: There's a rational explanation for everything that happens in the story. You can look at it as the kid just seeing these clowns, and the boy really *does* just drown. But at the end, when he goes into the bedroom and sees the clowns there, who is he killing? Of course, it *is* his parents' bed. If you look at it that way, the true horror is that he *sees* these clowns, but he's actually killing his parents.

But I wanted to leave that open to public questionability. I didn't want to tie it down.

Gardner Dozois: The question is, has he gone insane and just *thinks* he's seeing clowns, or is he really seeing clowns? And of course, as with the thing in "The Gods of Mars," it depends which way you collapse the wave-function. One possibility is that he's actually seeing these supernatural beings that are going around pushing people in front of buses, and then they come after him. The other way to look at it is, he's had a psychotic breakdown and is just making up all of these clowns as persecuting figures.

Susan Casper: I haven't looked at this story for a long time, but I seem to recall that I was very, very careful to make sure there was nothing tangible that the clowns did or left behind. That it was all the way possible from beginning to end that it was all in his head.

Gardner Dozois: Now, one potential weakness for this story is, we don't give a *reason* why he starts seeing clowns, in a supernatural sense. He doesn't blunder into an old Indian graveyard or something. He just suddenly starts seeing clowns. To my mind that makes it a little more likely that it's the psychotic breakdown explanation that's the valid one. There's no real reason that these clowns start haunting him, or that he starts to see them. You would think there would have to be a supernatural rationale for *why* he suddenly started seeing the clowns, and there really isn't one given.

Susan Casper: There was at that particular time period a great debate going on in the horror field between what had previously been foremost in horror, psychological horror, and what was coming to the front in the horror field, which was very tangible, very gory, very realistic, striking-with-the-knife kind of horror, dismembering people kind of horror. I had kind of wanted, within the boundaries of the story, to make a statement for the former. Because that's what I think is really scary.

Scary is in the head. It's not in the blood, it's not in the guts, it's not in seeing actual pieces of people lying on the ground. Horror is, as Bloch said in that story I mentioned about the clown, the out-of-place in the commonplace.

Gardner Dozois: We set up the possibility of it all being a psychotic break on the kid's part by mentioning that he had had psychological difficulties before. In fact, his parents are very embarrassed about him because he was a nut, basically, or had had psychological treatment of some sort, which in those days was a big stigmata. So that's all set up there, so you can if you wish interpret the story in that light.

At one point Susan and Jack and I actually sat down over dinner and were discussing doing a novel-length version of this story. But it didn't come to anything. Although I think it would have been possible.

Susan Casper: It would been, but I'm not sure anybody would have bought it.

Gardner Dozois: Well, that's another story. At the time, I think somebody might have. The big horror boom was underway then. Now, it's probably problematical.

I think what kept us from having any real enthusiasm for it was that you would have had to just plug more incidents into the same structure, rather than adding anything new in kind. You would have just had to plug in more incidents of him being chased around by clowns into the same basic structure.

Susan Casper: My basic objection to turning it into a novel is that I don't think we could have done it without putting out a real answer there. Yeah, the kid was crazy, or, yeah, there actually were clowns, and this is why they were following him around. I didn't particularly want to do either with it.

Gardner Dozois: Of course you could come up with a metaphysical structure where the clowns are *always* there, and every time somebody falls in front of a bus or falls down the stairs, it's because there was a clown there pushing them.

Susan Casper: The clown as death.

Gardner Dozois: Basically. Or the clown as malefic spirit, at any rate.

Susan Casper: The grim reaper in orange wig and funny nose.

Gardner Dozois: That's what the kid believes, at any rate.

Susan Casper: Anyway, I didn't want to tie it down. I didn't want to make it specific. I liked the story exactly the way it was. I like the fact that people were unsure whether or not it was actually happening or all in the kid's head. In fact, that's the main thing I get asked by people who've read the story: Was it real, or was it all in the kid's head? And, of course, the only thing you can say to that is, "Well, what do *you* think?"

Gardner Dozois: Actually, the bulk of the things that I've written, it's probably possible to ask the question, is it real or is it all inside the guy's head.

"SEND NO MONEY! The postcard said, in dark blue letters against a bright orange background. Judy smiled, and pushed it into the stack. She liked her junk mail. Certainly it was less depressing than the load of bills that made up the bulk of her mail. She especially liked the computer-generated "personalized" ones, eternally optimistic, that excitedly announced "You may have won a million dollars!" (Only Maybe Not), or the ones that promised to send you something "Absolutely Free!" for only $2 plus shipping and handling, or the ones that enclosed sample swatches of material, or paperthin slices of stale-looking fruitcake, or slightly squashed bits of cheese wrapped up in cellophane. Today's stack of junk mail was particularly large. Who knew what might be in it?"

"Send No Money" appeared in ISAAC ASIMOV'S SCIENCE FICTION MAGAZINE, the mid-December issue, 1985. With Shawna McCarthy, editor, right?

Gardner Dozois: Yep, Shawna McCarthy. In fact, that was almost the last story Shawna ever bought, before she gave up the editorship of the magazine. I think it might actually have *been* the last one she bought, in fact.

Was this the first collaboration you ever did with Susan?

Gardner Dozois: I *think* it was the first collaboration I did with her. She had started writing the story. The *idea* was hers. She had written a partial version, and then showed it to me because she was having trouble with it, and I ended up pretty much finishing the story with some input from her.

Once we had decided that the little people were behind this postcard campaign, the rest of it fell into place. What did the little people always want in payment? Your first-born child. It didn't seem that they would have changed that much, just because they had updated their sales pitch techniques. So we went with that. And once you say *that,* well, what would be a counter to that, which would end the story with an ironic twist? And that's what I used. So that she could have her cake and eat it too.

I didn't want the little people to win. There wouldn't have been enough of a snap to that.

Susan Casper: The way I remember it is I'd gotten an annoying piece of junk mail. I thought it said one thing, and then I picked up again and it turned out it actually said something else. And we started joking around about it. You know, personalized junk mail. The rest of it just flowed from there.

Gardner Dozois: Who did you think was responsible for the card? Did you have some entity or group in mind for producing it?

Susan Casper: The elves. In the traditional fairy tale sense.

Gardner Dozois: So *you're* the one who brought the elves in.

And the ending, I'm guessing is Susan's. Where it turns out that the protagonist has had her tubes tied, so she's pretty much content with the deal.

Susan Casper: Yes, that was pretty much mine. *He* wanted it to be cute, and so I came up with that.

Gardner Dozois: But you, from the start, had the idea that the fairies were behind it.

Susan Casper: The story was pretty much in place before you got involved in it. You just showed an interest in it, so we shared it. Unlike "The Stray," which you actually directed.

Gardner Dozois: The whole opening where Judy Pender is sitting there and being dissatisfied with her life and the postcard starts talking to her is basically Susan's. I threw in a couple of touches here and there. But primarily that was all Susan's idea.

Susan Casper: Once she meets the guy, I think it mostly becomes yours until we get to the ending. The dating business was mostly yours, as I recall.

Gardner Dozois: Well, there's really not a lot of dating business in it. He's never even actually named or described, I think. He might be named. But he's not an important character in the story.

I enjoyed writing the dialog of the card.

Susan Casper: Yeah, that was fun. That was the best part.

"You always think of unicorns as a horse with a horn, I reflected as it galloped past my window, and this *did* look quite a bit like a horse, but in some odd indefinable way it also looked just as much like a giant cat, or an otter, *or* a fox, or like any other sleek, smooth-furred, swift-moving, graceful creature. I opened the window, and leaned out for a better look. Yes, it was a unicorn, all right. It was silver (silver, not gray—there was a definite metallic sheen to its coat), with a cream-colored mane and tail. The single horn was gleaming white, and spiraled, and very long. In spite of the Unicorn Tapestry pictures, it had no fringy little billy-goat beard—in fact, a goat was one of the few sorts of creatures it *didn't* look like."

Let's go on to "The Stray." It appeared in THE TWI-LIGHT ZONE MAGAZINE, December 1987. A woman sees a unicorn, and it basically adopts her. It wants her to take it home.

Susan Casper: I started writing about the woman seeing a unicorn which she doesn't believe is a unicorn, Because she *wouldn't,* you know. Then I kind of got lost. And Gardner was reading it, and he kept giving me all of these suggestions, you should do this with it and you should do that with it. Finally, I just got disgusted with his suggestions, because I didn't particularly like any of them, and said, "Well then *you* write it!"

Gardner Dozois: I don't remember it this way. In fact, I remember you going to bed after we'd discussed this story, and while you were asleep, I wrote the rest of it.

Susan Casper: Yes, you did. You did! But after I said to you...

Gardner Dozois: And I showed it you as a *fait accompli,* somewhat nervously, the next morning.

Susan Casper: You were afraid I'd be pissed at you. That was because we had had this discussion, and you kept saying, "You should do this with it, you should do that with it." Which didn't feel right to me.

Gardner Dozois: I don't remember you saying, "Well, you write it."

Susan Casper: But I did. I said it jokingly. I didn't *seriously* mean for him to write the story. But what can I tell you? You've got to be careful what you say to a writer.

Gardner Dozois: It seemed to call for a sentimental ending. I didn't see anywhere we could sell it, if it didn't have a sentimental ending. The ending was perhaps more sentimental than either of us was...

Susan Casper: ...was comfortable with?

Gardner Dozois: ...really comfortable with. But it wasn't the kind of story that would have supported a snapper ending, where the unicorn rips her throat out or something.

Susan Casper: I started out playing with the idea of a fantasy creature in the real world, and how someone might react to a fantasy creature in the real world. Of course, the first reaction that came to me was total disbelief: I've seen something else. It only *looked* like a unicorn.

Whose idea was it to equate unicorns with cats?

Gardner Dozois: Well, it was cute, so that was probably my idea. I kept wanting the story to be cuter than Susan really wanted it to be. But I thought naked sentimentality was our only chance of making this story saleable. And I think actually I was right in that call. I don't see how else it could have ended.

You have to keep distracting the reader from the hordes of real-world problems that would arise in this situation. Which in fact, I believe we actually mention in the story and then dismiss. Like, having a horse in your rec room is not a really good idea.

Susan Casper: On the other hand, we set it up that this one didn't eat, and therefore didn't defecate, didn't make a mess.

Gardner Dozois: She keeps asking, "Why did you pick *me?* I'm not a virgin." And obviously the reason the unicorn picks her is so that she can have her kittens in her closet, because she's a nice person. So that was my answer. She couldn't find any virgins who would let her have kittens in *their* closets.

Susan Casper: Being disillusioned with men was obviously something that she and the unicorn had in common.

Let me ask you this, Gardner. Would you have been willing to be that sentimental in a story that had only your name on it, and not Susan's to hide behind?

Gardner Dozois: Probably not. 'Cause everybody can blame Susan. "Oh, well, there's that yucky girl stuff that girls like to put into a story." I really couldn't think of any other practical ending for the story, though. The tone from the start would not have supported a turnaround twist ending in which the unicorn rips her stomach out with its horn.

Susan Casper: That wasn't what I had in mind.

Gardner Dozois: I mean, you couldn't go to that kind of an ending. It *had* to be a sentimental ending. And once having committed to a sentimental ending, I figured you might as well pull out all the stops and make it as sentimental as possible.

Susan Casper: Originally, I had been playing more with the idea of here she was with a fantasy creature in the real world, and, of course, it could only get her in trouble. Not that it would harm her, but that it would obviously get her in trouble of some sort without meaning to. But I got bogged down. I couldn't figure out where to take it, and that's where he came in.

Gardner Dozois: You wrote a long scene which we later had to take out, with the unicorn rampaging around the supermarket and knocking all the groceries off the shelf.

Susan Casper: Following her, yeah.

Gardner Dozois: That was the kind of trouble there it was going to get her into. But it just didn't seem fantasy-ish enough, somehow. It could've been a big dog following her around.

Susan Casper: And *we* didn't throw it out. I seem to recall I didn't get a vote.

Gardner Dozois: Well, you went to bed! You let me finish the story. That was your mistake, right there.
I don't think it's a particularly major story. It's got a couple of cute points in it. If we hadn't sold it to THE TWILIGHT ZONE MAGAZINE, we probably could have sold it to some children's or YA fantasy anthology. We could probably still sell it today. There's always a market for this kind of story.

Susan Casper: I actually had a lot more vested in "Send No Money," which I thought was the much better of the two stories, myself.

―――――――――――――――――――――

"Kleisterman took a zeppelin to Denver, a feeder line to Pueblo, then transferred to a clattering local bus to Santa Fe. The bus was full of displaced Anglos who preferred the life of migrant fieldworker to the Oklahoma refugee camps, a few Cambodians, a few Indians, and a number of the poorer Hispanics, mostly *mestizos*—unemployables who had hoped that the liberation would mean the fulfillment of all their dreams, but who had instead merely found themselves working for rich Mexican *caudillos* rather than for millionaire Anglos. Most of the passengers had been across the border to blow their work vouchers in Denver or Cañon City, and were now on their way back into Aztlan for another week's picking. They slouched sullenly in their seats, some passed out from drink or God Food and already snoring, many wrapped in ponchos or old Army blankets against the increasing chill of the evening. They ignored Kleisterman, even though, in spite of his carefully anonymous clothes, he was clearly no field hand—and Kleisterman preferred it that way."

"Solace" appeared in the February 1990 issue of OMNI. This is certainly an odd story.

Gardner Dozois: It's a story with a curious origin. It's one of several stories I've written which originated at base in a dream. One night I had the dream which is basically the core of the story, where a guy comes in to the doctor who has the simulator machine and asks him to destroy him, and he is destroyed psychologically, and he doesn't know at the end whether or not he actually is still in the machine or not. I remembered this and wrote it down the next day. The exercise of craft thereafter was to work backward to rationalize a physical real-world structure wherein this could happen.

Rather than starting the story with him walking into the doctor's office, which seemed to me too abrupt, I started it back with him getting on a bus and going toward the place where he was going to meet the doctor. Taking him toward the office in slow increments.

I could have set it anywhere, I suppose. I happened to pick Santa Fe because I had been to Santa Fe fairly recently and knew the local color. Because it *had* interesting local color. It occurred to me when I was playing around with possible settings for the story that there were a couple of interesting touches I could work into the background if I used Santa Fe, like the Mexicans reconquering Aztlan and turning Anglos into migrant field workers. They're not really important to the story, but they contribute a nice sense of verisimilitude for the world. Once you have the core idea, though, the story could have been set anywhere. I could have set it in Philadelphia or New Jersey or New York or anywhere else. But the background that I finally *did* pick seemed more interesting and more exotic to me. It clearly shares a few background details with other stories such as "Apres Moi" and "A Knight of Ghosts and Shadows," as well as with my unfinished novel *Nottamun Town,* and perhaps even with "The Peacemaker." If I'd somehow managed to finish a novel in the '90s, this probably would have been the background setting. Or a similar one, anyway.

The whole outer part of the story, though, is just basically a mechanism to get Kleisterman into that doctor's office, to set up a few foreshadowings and clues of various sorts, and to create a little bit of the sense of the character and how he's haunted and obsessed.

My *own* opinion, which I stress again is just my opinion and not necessarily what the story "really" is about, is that he's been in a simulator machine from before the opening of the story. And is still in one at the end. Which he's beginning to suspect, although he tries to deny it at the end.

So there are really three possible readings. One is what ostensibly happens, the second is that he's in a machine from the beginning, and the third would be that when he goes in to be destroyed, he *is* destroyed and everything after that is a simulation.

Gardner Dozois: Yes, and I think that each of those interpretations is equally valid. There's not any real hard evidence to point one way or the other for any of them.

Now, there's a couple of very subtle things I put in that *I* take as clues that he's in a simulator from the beginning. For instance, when he gets to Santa Fe, he throws in a mention that the food tastes like chalk and ashes, and that all food has tasted terrible to him for months. In my mind, this is an indication that he's being punished in a simulator. But who knows? It could just be that the diner has crappy food.

I notice that the ostensible plot does not begin until Kleisterman walks into the office, and that happens on page seven of a ten page story.

Gardner Dozois: Yeah, this is how to keep your audience riveted, and is why I have shot to the top of the best-seller list, along with Stephen King and John Grisham and Tom Clancy. Actually, what was most important in my mind was not the rather perfunctory plot, but the fact of his psychological mood. Which I tried to bring out by the way he's reacting to things on his bus trip, and the fact that he's afraid to sleep. The fact that he sees his dead girlfriend standing outside the bus. Several similar moments.

Of course, this gets into Phil Dick territory in a way, in that he can't ever be *sure* that the world is actually real. Once he has this suspicion enter his mind, there's no way he can actually prove to himself that what he's going through is reality. There are even a couple of minutes when he tries to prove to himself that this is really happening by examining stuff around him in as much physical detail as possible, saying, "Well, surely they couldn't get *this* kind of detail!" But in the back of his head he knows that actually they probably *could* get this kind of detail. So it doesn't really give him any kind of ease psychologically. And of course, as Phil Dick repeatedly demonstrated, this is true of all of *us* as well. I mean, we have no way to prove that the world around us is actually real. It's probably best not to think about that. Just put it out of your mind altogether. Once you start down that road, there's no place to stop.

For better or worse, I think we're better off just accepting that the world is real and just not worrying about it. Call it trust, call it denial, whichever you will. This, however, is not an option given to Kleisterman.

I know you hate my exegetic readings of your work, but I can't help but notice that the doctor, Dr. Au, has a name

which is the elemental symbol for gold, and also is pronounced as "Ow," like a small cry of pain. Is any of that intended?

Gardner Dozois: Your readings of my stories are always so much cleverer than the stories themselves that it's always disappointing to straighten you out...
Actually, though, that is intentional. Not so much the reference to gold, although he is a man who's trying to get rich by running an illicit service, but the cry of pain, the Au being pronounced as "Ow," that was intentional. In fact, it came from a sign that existed for many years in Chinatown, here in Philadelphia. Which I noticed and commented on a number of occasions when I was walking by with various people. It said, "Dr. Au—Painless Dentist." Which I though was quite amusing. So I stole his name for the doctor in this story.

___

"Allen and I were cousins, and we grew up within a few blocks of each other in a sleepy neighborhood in Mount Airey. We were never close—at first, he didn't like girls, and then later, when he did, our consanguinity caused him to seek elsewhere for female companionship—but we saw a lot of each other. Too much, I sometimes thought, although there were times when Allen could be charming and entertaining, even to girls—especially if there were grown-ups around to watch."

___

"Apres Moi" appeared in the November issue of OMNI in that same year. This is the story of young Allen, who got away with everything. I recall you once said that when you

got the idea, the first thing you did was to go around and ask everyone you knew what things people had gotten away with in their lives.

Gardner Dozois: Yes, that's true, I did. I believe I even asked you and Marianne, though which specific things you said people had gotten away with, I don't recall. I certainly asked Susan, and anyone else who was around during the period where I was writing this story.

In fact, there's quite a lot of things that people get away with that other people are still resentful of decades later, even if it's something as minor as them having to do the dishes instead of somebody else. You probably take this stuff to the grave with you.

Susan, do you remember which bit I stole from you for "Apres Moi"?

Susan Casper: It was about getting out of doing the dishes *and* getting the piece of chocolate cake.

Gardner Dozois: Whoop! See? Decades later, and she's still bitter about not getting that piece of chocolate cake!

This is another trick story in that ostensibly the narrator is just reminiscing about this guy who always got away with everything, but then, right at the end, the perspective draws back to reveal a different sort of story. He'd died young and therefore he'd missed seeing the country go to hell. Ending with a horrific little description of the world this woman lives in, and the pain and misery she has to endure.

Gardner Dozois: What I was toying with here was how the perception of things can change. Originally, people greet the news of Allen's death with, "Oh, that's too bad!" and other such ritual sounds you automatically make on such occasions. But then it occurs to the protagonist at the end that Allen's actually *lucky* to have died when he did. By dying, he's gotten out of going through all these horrors that she has to go through.

If I recall correctly, the origin of this story was that one morning I was getting ready to go to work in New York, and there was some ominous environmental news on the TV about holes in the Antarctic ozone layer, the coming ecological collapse, or something like that, and everybody was being very grim and shaking their heads. It occurred to me then that if the future they were projecting was actually going to come to pass, that I might be *lucky* if the train crashed on the way to work and killed me, so that I wouldn't have to go through all of this.

Working from there, I came up with the ironic twist of the man who had gotten *out* of everything in his entire life, and finally gets out of having to lead this horrible existence by what seems initially like a tragic turn of fate instead. Him being killed in the crash seems like his comeuppance, but actually it's not, because he gets *out* of everything once again.

Among the list of sources for the world's ills, the air-vectored AIDS and the purges and the cholera and so on, you have the rise of Chiliastic cults. So basically you're saying that this is all happening, oh, about last year.

Gardner Dozois: Yeah, probably. It turned out to be a little premature in its predictions. But I did write this well before the actual turn of the Millennium. But, of course, we haven't actually gotten to the turn of the Millennium *yet*, if you talk to the calendar purists. So we have time to squeeze all this stuff in between now and 2001.

Another irony I was playing with here was how really good most Americans have had it, and have it still, although we constantly gripe and complain. We live better than kings did in most eras. I go through the list there. A typical middle class American—this doesn't apply to someone lying on a hot air vent, of course—can drive anywhere he wants to in his own personal automobile that can take him across the country at great speed. He doesn't have to file travel plans or carry internal passports or visas. He can eat anything he wants at any time he wants, including exotic dishes that emperors in some eras at some times couldn't get. Fresh fruit in the winter! He can have light come on by flicking a button, he can have as much water as he wants come out of a tap in the wall whenever he wants it. He can take a bath whenever he wants to. He can make it cool in the summer and hot in the winter just by turning a dial. It's really a pretty luxurious life that people are living here, at least in the West at the beginning of the twenty-first century.

Even the poor people, except for the guy on the hot air vent, probably live better than most rich people did three or four hundred years ago. I don't think people appreciate how well they're actually living, or how precarious it all is. How easy it would be to lose all of that, and be an old fart somewhere saying, "When I was a boy, you could turn a switch and lights would come on!" and they'd say, "Oh, Grandpa, blow it out your ass! You're such a liar!"

It could all vanish very easily. That's part of what I was getting at in the story.

"Sven left the midnight forest, and turned down the slope toward the sea. Where the tall sea grass ended and the path slanted down the shingle toward the beach, he stopped to put his dark-lantern down on the hard-packed scree; he dared not take it near Them. He plunged his dagger to the hilt into the ground, next to the lantern. Nor cold iron. He shifted the weight of the bag on his shoulder and continued down the path."

"Passage" appeared in 1993, in *Xanadu*, edited by Jane Yolen. This was another story inspired by a dream?

Gardner Dozois: Yes, this is another dream story. The dream section is at the end, where Sven goes into the Elven ship and gives his sack to the Elf and the Elf tells him he wants him now to go off and get a bag of hearts. That basically was the dream. The rest of it was rationalizing the framework, as with "Solace." Again, I started the guy back up the hill above the beach, rather than starting the story with him walking into the ship. I had him walk down the hill, rid himself of his cold iron and other things that the Elves wouldn't like, and walk down the beach to the ship to give myself more time to build up atmosphere, to give some indication of the character's psychological state, and to build up a bit of anticipation of what was going to happen to him. Which I didn't think I could do if I started with him just walking into the ship in the first paragraph of the first page.

But what *happens* in the ship is pretty much how I dreamed it. It didn't make a lot of sense to me in my dream, and it didn't make a lot of sense to me when I woke up, and it didn't make a lot of sense to me afterwards either. But there was a dream-logic there that was somehow attractive. So, rather than try to come up with a rationale for it, I just left it there as dream-logic. After all, you're dealing with Faerie, with the irrational side of the world. The dreaming pole. It didn't seem to me that what they wanted him to do would *have* to make a lot of sense.

Obviously, if he had gotten the bag of heads for them, he could have gotten them the bag of hearts at the same time, if you want to look at it realistically. But I think what's coming across here is they're giving him a task to do, and it's essentially meaningless. Arbitrary. Perhaps the *point* is that it's meaningless and arbitrary. It's just something he has to do to pay the price of passage. Maybe to prove that he *wants* it enough to deserve it. They could have told him to go out and get a thousand caterpillars and it wouldn't make any difference. But, being rather dark beings, they tell him to go out and kill a whole bunch more people and get their hearts.

What this all means psychologically, I'm not sure. I'm sure a Freudian could analyze this and discover the most dreadful things about me. But that's the dream the way it came out.

The imagery in the descriptive passages seems to me to be stone fantasy. Not just beautiful imagery, but fantastic. The elf has a voice "like a bell ringing under ice," and Sven makes the Sign of the White Christ, and then Thor's Hammer, and so on.

Gardner Dozois: It was obviously a fantasy story. There was no way I could rationalize it as science fiction. Perhaps because as a story based on dream-logic, it didn't really make any sense in the first place. So it needed to be fantasy.

I'm pretty sure I didn't have a specific picture in mind of what the guy giving the bag of heads to the Elf looked like in my dream. So I thought, well, what kind of a character would be coming to trade human body parts for passage on a ship to Fairie. Obviously it wasn't a modern character. Why I settled on a Norseman in particular I'm not sure, except that I knew a little about that background. Enough to work in things like the reference to making Thor's Hammer. It's a background that has always appealed to me, so perhaps that's why I instinctively used that particular background.

Jane felt that it wasn't made specific enough that he was a Norseman. So she wanted me to add a line about the wind ruffling his beard. Which seemed harmless enough to me, so I did. Although it already seemed obvious enough to me from the rest of the references that he was a Norseman.

The thing I had a lot of trouble getting people to understand—I'm not even sure it's correct in the final text—is when he hears the barking of a scrannel dog. The word "scrannel" seems to have gone out of the language. Not only did Jane change it to something else, but all of the subsequent copy editors kept changing it to other things. I guess nobody understands what scrannel means anymore. I don't even know if it came across right in the published version.

Here's the passage.

Gardner Dozois: By God, it *didn't!* What it says here is, "and hear the scrannel yapping of a dog." Which doesn't make sense. For the record, it should be "and hear the yapping of a scrannel dog."

It seems strange to see you writing core fantasy...

Gardner Dozois: I don't know if there's a lot to say about this story really. The atmosphere of the dream was creepy, and I tried to reproduce that. I always thought that, although perhaps beautiful, Elves would *also* be terrible and enigmatic and rather frightening. They're not human, after all, and their motivations and goals and passions are not those of a human being. So while we might admire them for their beauty, they're not really benign creatures. They're ruled by whims and caprices that to *us* are enigmatic and often cruel and perhaps even deadly.

Whether I would have bothered to have actually sat down and written this out if *Xanadu* hadn't been open as a fantasy market, I am not sure. You can consider it a little glimpse of an alternative career for me. If I'd become a writer of fantasy novels, this is what they would have come out like.

Anything else?

Gardner Dozois: One of the physical details I remember from the dream was the kinetic memory of the heads shifting around inside the bag as he handed it over. That got into the story.

Being Gardner Dozois

I think it's possible, it suddenly occurs to me, although I don't remember one hundred percent at this point, that in the dream the Elf asks for a bag of eyes, rather than hearts, and that I changed it to hearts as being more easily comprehensible. If *that* is true, and I think it might be, then the story probably owes a debt, way back in my subconscious, to a Jack Vance story where Chun the Unavoidable wants people to bring him golden eyes to put into his tapestry. So it's quite possible that that was a heretofore unsuspected ancestor of the story from way back in the bubbling depths of my subconscious mind somewhere.

"It was high summer in Orange, in York, in the Human Domain of Earth. There was commerce in the town, crops in the field, beasts in the byre, bandits in the roads, thants and chimeras in the hills, and God in His Heaven—which was fifteen miles away, due east."

We now come to "The City of God," written with my humble assistance, which appeared in 1995 in OMNI ONLINE, Ellen Datlow, fiction editor, and had its first print publication in the October/November 1996 issue of ASIMOV'S SCIENCE FICTION, editor—you.

Gardner Dozois: I discretely offered it to Sheila Williams, rather than myself, and she made the decision as to whether they would take it or not.

This is a very old story in its origins. I met you in 1974, and back then the partially-written manuscript was legendary among your friends, who referred to it as "The Digger Novel."

Gardner Dozois: I started this story all the way back in a very, very hot summer night in 1970, much like the night described early on in the story, when I was living in New York City, in a slum apartment on the Lower East Side. It flowed very well and easily up until the point where the protagonist, Hanson, crosses the bridge away from his old life towards whatever is going to be his new life. At that point, it faltered and ran dry. I think the problem was that, though I had no difficulty picturing in great detail his old life of squalor and misery, I didn't have imagination enough to picture what his fabulous new life was like.

I had sketched out in my mind some scenes where he was walking around on the other side of the Wall. But they weren't very interesting. Even I dimly realized this at the time. My beyond-the-Wall society would have been something like a snazzy shopping mall with rich, bored immortals walking around in it. Maybe like something out of the movie *Logan's Run*. It obviously was not good enough.

I heard references to this, whispers in the jungle, expressions of awe from Susan and Jack and others who had actually seen it for years before I actually saw it. I knew that I had passed some kind of threshold as your friend one time when Susan asked you to go out for cigarettes, and you went back to get your coat and emerged carrying the manuscript in a cardboard box. You dropped it in my lap and said, "Here, Michael, you can read this while I'm gone."

Which left me stunned for two reasons. First, because you trusted me enough to let me read it. Secondly, because you were going all the way to the corner and back, and wouldn't be gone for more than four minutes. So I had enough time to read a page and a half before you took it out of my hands and put it back in the closet.

Gardner Dozois: [Laughs]

Years later, after I'd finally read it, Jack Dann and I spent an evening throwing ideas at you for what could be on the other side of the Wall when Hanson goes into the City of God. We enthusiastically spun out idea after idea, and you'd listen carefully, then hunch your head down and give it a little shake. Obviously the hind-brain knew what it wanted done with the story, and was saying, "Nope. That's not it."

Gardner Dozois: It's clear I didn't have the imagination to come up with what the City of God was going to be like and have it actually be interesting. I had no difficulty picturing the squalid, decayed environment of Orange because it was basically just an exaggeration and fabulation of the kind of life that I was used to living. But having been brought up poor, and having lived mostly in poor districts all my life, I don't think I had the experiences in the tank, the referents, to really picture what the *other* side of the Wall would be like. Everything I did come up with was unconvincing, even to me.

I think what the story really needed, and which you provided, was a big blast of high-imagination Special Effects. Once you provided that, the story flowed fairly easily to its conclusion. We needed those high-color, high-energy Special Effects that you blasted in there.

I got involved with this, I think it was in 1994. Quite a lot of time had passed. I was visiting you, and as I got up to leave, you said, "Wait a second," disappeared into the back room, and returned with the same cardboard box of manuscript. You handed it to me, and said, "Here, Michael. I'm obviously not going to do anything with this. Why don't you turn it into a novella?"

I immediately said, "Oh, this is incredible, Gardner, because I've got a great idea for how the rest of this should go. I'm not going to tell you right now—I'm going to surprise you." Could you tell I was lying?

Gardner Dozois: No, I'm pretty naïve and trusting. I was confident you could do something with it. I frankly would have liked to finish it myself, having started it, but it became clear after more than twenty-five years that I was never going to finish it. So I figured that if it was ever going to see print in any form before I died, I probably had better turn to the assistance of my friends.

I wouldn't have touched it, if I'd thought there was any chance you'd finish it yourself. I must say that, although I believe that the parts I wrote do not shame you, nevertheless all the best stuff was written by you. Particularly the very opening, where Hanson is shoveling coal into a hole. He does this for page after page, nothing but shoveling coal into a hole. Yet it is riveting, and in that passage his life is revealed and then destroyed, before your very eyes. After which there's absolutely no point in going on, and yet he *does* go on. It was a bravura piece of writing. It still knocks me out. And although I'm pleased with the special effects that I put in—I think they were worthy of Industrial Light and Magic, in their way—still, that's all they were. The important stuff in the story occurs inside Hanson's head.

Gardner Dozois: I did draw on my own experience, of course. I have shoveled coal in road gangs in the Army on a couple of occasions, a not terribly pleasant job, and that's obviously in there. The opening part of the story in particular probably owes a major debt to Edgar Pangborn, as at least one critic, Greg Feeley, has been astute enough to notice. I was heavily influenced by Pangborn's *Davy* when I wrote that section. It probably influenced the setting, and influenced the dialect that they used, and probably influenced it on several other levels as well. So that's probably the major discernable influence there.

The post-Utopian York feels a lot to me like mid-state post-

industrial New York. Having grown up there, I felt enormous surges of nostalgia reading this.

Gardner Dozois: I decided to set it in Orange just because, when I first moved down here from New York City, we were driving around at one point, and I came across Orange and West Orange and East Orange, and Orange just seemed like an amusing name for a town. It stuck in my head. So I decided to use it.

At one point, I had gotten a map and drawn lines on it to show the extent of the Wall of the City of God. But I don't have that anymore.

I always knew that the adventure had to take Hanson over the Wall and into the City of God and that something had to happen to him there of a transmutive nature. But I never could get him over the Wall.

When you handed the story to me, the last thing you said was, "But leave it open-ended, in case we decide to make a novel." I immediately said, "You're reading my mind!" But in that instant, I immediately saw how to resolve the problem. Which was that when he gets to the other side, there's nobody there. The City of God is empty. Which brings it back to mythological territory. If there had been decadent people wandering around, that would have been difficult to achieve.

Gardner Dozois: I do know that in my head I had a scene where the decadent people casually cure him of cancer by a simple flick of a high-tech button. So I knew that had to be in there somewhere.

I think your most brilliant contribution to this, besides the special effects that paint the picture of what the City of God is like, was the whole idea of the key that the other guy is carrying in his body. The scene where it plunges *out* of him and *into* Hanson took me completely by surprise when I was reading what you'd done with the story. But it seemed perfectly right and appropriate. In fact, I don't think the rest of the story could have functioned without it. So that was inspired.

When I was writing it, I discovered that the way to collaborate with you is exactly the opposite of how to collaborate with Bill Gibson. When he and I were working on "Dogfight," I came to a scene that cried out for Gibson to write it. But since it was my turn with the manuscript, I figured I'd just write a lame-ass version of it, which he would fix up. But to my horror, he wrote back very enthusiastically about that scene—obviously, he'd been waiting for me to do *something* right—and hadn't changed a word. I had to bust a gut to bring that section up to Gibson standards because everyone would've assumed he'd written it, and that he'd lost his ability to write well.

So when I began this collaboration, I mostly stayed away from writing a Gardner Dozois kind of prose. But at some point I found that ersatz Dozois really bugged the hell out of you. You'd stay up all night feverishly rewriting it, until it felt right to you. The Michael Swanwick prose you were perfectly happy to let slide.

Gardner Dozois: I did go over your draft and burnish it lightly here and there.

No, you reworked it very thoroughly. Not that I minded.

Gardner Dozois: I did add a retrospective passage to the penultimate scene in the story, where Hanson is sitting on the throne in the City of God and he's looking back over his life and musing on it, and remembering looking at a diorama in the Courthouse in the City of Orange when he was a boy. Which would probably have been more effective if I had mentioned that originally, in the opening of the story. But *c'est la vie*.

I did want to get that reflective-introspective-retrospective feeling into that passage, though. A summing-up. And I feathered it over a bit here and there, where I thought maybe the joins were a little obvious. But I think it worked out fairly seamlessly, actually.

I was happy with this. I was particularly pleased that a couple of the critics, who were very perceptive readers, told me they couldn't find the break-point in the story, where your prose left off and mine began. Which I would've thought was fairly obvious because it breaks when Hanson passes through the Wall.

Gardner Dozois: I believe that the divide actually comes not when he goes through the Wall, but somewhat earlier, because you introduced Boone as a character. Boone was your character and not mine.

You provided a manuscript that ran from the beginning of the story through the point where Hanson obviously has to pass through the Wall. When I took it on, I handled it the only way possible, by giving myself carte blanche to change the characters, the plot, the prose, to throw in a dancing moose if I felt like it, anything at all. I ran it through the typewriter a couple of times. There were a couple of pages that I threw out, right at the very end, where you had him just traveling on some more...

Gardner Dozois: That's where I started to run dry on this story.

Those pages were hesitation marks. He had to pass over to the other side.

Gardner Dozois: It worked fine until he crosses the bridge over the Hudson. As he's going across the Hudson, there's a fairly lyrical passage about him crossing the bridge, and the sun is coming up, and his whole life is falling away behind him, and his new life is looming up ahead of him...I think, in a way, I painted myself into a corner with that. Because I had written that passage so well, with such a feeling of finality, this is his life coming to an end, that I sort of ran out of steam about what to do with his new life that was starting on the other side of the river.

I did go on for a few pages after that. But it began increasingly to feel like wheel-spinning. He was doing the same things he had done on the other side of the river. He was riding on the road-tractor, and looking around...

Except for those pages, which I believe I worked into the remaining material...

Gardner Dozois: You worked a little of it in. But primarily the dividing point is when he crosses the bridge over the Hudson. From then on in, it's primarily your stuff.

Up to that point, I believe I may have changed one word. But then again, I may have changed the word and then decided I was wrong and changed it back. We'll never quite know. But that entire opening section was so thoroughly worked that it did not admit to change without turning it into something else. You couldn't improve it, you could just turn it into some other story.

Gardner Dozois: In a way, that may be why I was never able to finish it. Because it came to an emotional stopping point. Yeah, he still has cancer. Yeah, he doesn't know what's going to happen on the other side of the river. But it almost felt subconsciously as though when he crossed the river, he'd come to the end of his journey. To an emotional stopping-point. So my subconscious said, "Oh, okay, well *that's* done!" and just shut down the shop.

I hate the subconscious.

Gardner Dozois: "We don't have to worry about *that* anymore! Finished that one. I'm going to go out and have lunch now. Would you like me to bring you a sandwich?"

Obnoxious little bastard!

Gardner Dozois: That's the sort of thing the subconscious does. When it decides to stop working on a project, it's very difficult to coax it into working on it again. So I think that may have been part of the problem. And lack of imagination on my part. I do think it was a collaboration where our skills were complimentary. In that what was needed to finish the story was what you could provide to it. I had already pretty much contributed my part. It dovetailed pretty well with what you did.

Did you notice that at the very end I quoted Friedrich Nietzsche? When the soldier asks him if he's seen God, and Hanson cries, "You fool! God is dead!" That's from *Also Sprach Zarathustra*. Which I thought was a pretty good joke, considering that there cannot be less of an *Ubermensch* Nietzschean individual than Hanson.

Gardner Dozois: Hanson is not really impressed with himself, that's part of his problem. But he sort of always manages to do the right thing, even though it takes him a long time to grind his way through to it. He's fundamentally a decent individual. Not very bright, and aware that he's not very bright. But he keeps handing power to people who are much brighter than him, and they keep misusing it terribly.

I like Hanson a lot. He never for an instant believes he ever does the right thing. He wanders along, in fact, doing the

best possible thing—including killing his supervisor, who definitely had it coming—and then feeling guilty. I don't think he ever does the right thing without feeling guilty about it.

Gardner Dozois: He always tries to get other people to do the things he knows that need to be done, because he knows they're smarter and better than him. Yet somehow they keep fucking it up, and handing the power and the responsibility back to *him* instead. So he finally has to accept that and do the best that he can. He has no idea at the end, when he opens the City of God, whether this is the right thing to do or not. He just knows that if he doesn't do it now, that it's never going to happen, and the status quo is going to prevail until the end of time. He takes a chance. But he's certainly not sure that he's doing the right thing.

I'll mention here, without going into any detail, that you have in your mind how the novel would end. After many complex and not-yet-invented travails, Hanson will finally find peace. Hard though that might be to believe.

Gardner Dozois: I think he would find peace because...He would be handed power, and he would keep it reluctantly, because he had no choice, but he wouldn't think he was worthy of it. This is a riff I probably got out of Tolkien. In Tolkien, almost all the major characters are offered the ring, and they all shrink away from actually taking it. It's probably the only fantasy where people try to get *rid of* and not assume power, rather than trying to gain as much power as possible.

It's hard to talk about a novel that hasn't been written yet. That may never be. But I dimly see Hanson as ultimately being left with some sort of gatekeeper or overseer responsibility for the rest of humanity that he didn't really want, and didn't really think he was doing a good job at. But he would feel he had no choice but to shoulder the burden.

Your version of the City of God is like...I think I see bits in there of Brian Aldiss's story "Old Hundredth."

Actually, the idea is a change on the Strugatskys' *Roadside Picnic*. Wherein aliens have visited the Soviet Union and left a lot of very dangerous stuff behind. People go in, risking their lives for the enormous potential gain, but knowing at the same time they run the risk of being worked over by the alien technology in ways that cannot be anticipated and may be extremely unpleasant.

Gardner Dozois: I thought that the fact that all of the people had disappeared, and the way that the constructs that had been left behind could not be explained, was reminiscent of the theme in Aldiss's story, where the people had transformed themselves into a strange form that the creatures left behind could not understand.

Ah, but that was a transcendent form! I figured from your setup, where the rich people had built themselves a walled community—this was before gated communities, by the way—and retreated within and let the rest of the world fall apart, though they could easily fix things up themselves...

Gardner Dozois: Actually it *wasn't* before gated communities. I used to visit Jack Dann when he lived in Sea Gate in Brooklyn, right at the tip of Coney Island, which was a gated community. You had to show a visitor's card before they would let you in. So this is not as new an idea as you perhaps think.

But it did seem to me that whatever had happened to the rich people, they had not gone on to a godlike transcendent state. Somehow or other they'd killed themselves off. But they'd managed to keep their toys from falling into the hands of the rabble anyway.

Gardner Dozois: Of course, it's a very working-class story in some ways. Not only because of my own working-class origins, but because he's laboring as a factory worker. And, of course, I knew lots of factory workers when I was growing up. His own self-deprecation, where he keeps referring to himself as a dumb ox, and a slob, and talking about how other people are much smarter and better than he is, is part of the psychological mind set which is created to keep the workers down, basically. There is a sort of a labor-versus-management subtext that runs throughout the story.

It crackles with class hatred.

Gardner Dozois: There's a bit at the end, which I believe I put in after you had done your draft, where Hanson talks about how his friend Boone has now turned himself into a boss. You work your entire life next to somebody, and he's just as downtrodden as you, and then he gets a promotion, and he turns into a *boss,* and he begins grinding *your* face into the dirt, just as other people were once grinding *his* face into the dirt. That's quite deliberately put in there.

I think that if Hanson ever was given the ultimate power, as indeed he is given it for a few minutes at the end of the story, the thing that might keep him from being *too* destructive with it is this horror that he might himself turn into a boss. That's the last thing he wants to do is to turn into a boss. Because he's seen that from the other side.

And of course it's the only thing Hanson has got. At the end, everything has been taken away from him except his basic decency. If he loses that, he doesn't have anything.

Gardner Dozois: Hanson could quite possibly become as corrupt as anybody else. The only thing that keeps him from becoming as corrupt as everybody else is this knowledge of how bad it looks from the lower depths when you allow yourself to be transformed into a boss, and sort of a determination to not have that happen to him. So he has the ultimate power for a short time, but what he basically does is give it away. Rather than manipulate things for his own aggrandizement, as Boone would have done, he opens up the City of God, and says, "There. You now have a chance to make what you will make of the world." He has no way of knowing if it will be bad, worse than the current situation, or good, will improve things. It's a crap shoot. He's basically saying, "Here's your chance." Rather than keeping the power for himself, he's opening it up to everybody else back in the real world.

I suppose there's probably a hint of Gully Foyle in there, where he gives the PyrE to the crowd, rather than keeping it for an elite group of scientists to manipulate. There's something that appeals to me in that. Although the chances are good that somebody in the crowd is going to take the PyrE and blow up the universe. Still, the elite scientists and politicians would probably end up blowing up the universe *too*. At least you're giving the sensibility of ordinary people a chance. Whether they'll rise to the occasion or not is another matter. But I don't think we're any better off with the elite running things.

That winds up my questions. Can you think of anything else to add?

Gardner Dozois: I probably should add, before we move away from "The City of God," that the title was yours. Although I refer constantly to the City of God in the story, the story itself never was titled until we finished the collaboration. It was referred to as "The Digger Story."

I came up with this as a working title. I didn't really want to use it because it's the same as the title of St. Augustine's famous book, and it didn't really refer back to that work.

But you said, "Oh, go ahead. He can watch out for himself."

Gardner Dozois: He's a saint, after all. He's got it made in his cushy job in Heaven.

It seemed appropriate enough. It *is* a phrase that is used throughout the story. I probably was too dumb and uneducated to have heard of St. Augustine's *The City of God*, but I got the phrase from someplace, out of the depths of my subconscious. It might as easily have been that as anything else.

"Darkness. The smell of grass, and wet earth, and fog. The night moved through the clearing like a river. A few distant pinpricks of stars overhead, faint and far and pale. Somewhere down the hill, the grass rustled as a mouse fled through it, but the People were not hunting tonight."

Going from "The City of God," which is one of your major works, to perhaps one of your less-major works, which is "A Cat Horror Story"...

Gardner Dozois: I can think of less major stories of mine than *that* without any difficulties whatsoever.

Now this was published in THE MAGAZINE OF FANTASY AND SCIENCE FICTION, November 1994, edited by Kristine Kathryn Rusch. This is really a gimmick story. It's a one-joke story, I think it's fair to say—or am I wrong here?

Gardner Dozois: Actually, I think in some ways it's more substantial than some of my *other* masterpieces of modern science fiction. If I had to pick being remembered by posterity for this or for "The Mayan Variation," for instance, I would take this in a shot.

Yeah, it's a minor story. I think it does some good work for what it is. There are some interesting touches in it. It's a story that goes over well if you read it to an audience. Audiences really seem to like it, which must count for something.

It may look a little better when compared to the overall subgenre of science fiction cat stories. Since I have edited two anthologies of science fiction cat stories, I know what the competition is in this particular area. And I must say that, although I don't like to be seen patting myself on the back, it's probably better than *most* science fiction and fantasy cat stories, with the notable exception of "Space-Time for Springers" by Fritz Leiber. Who practically invented the whole sub-subgenre in the first place.

This had a very specific origin in that Ellen Datlow was editing an anthology of horror stories about cats. She called me up at one point and asked me to write a cat horror story, and I said, "Well, okay, I guess." I don't do well, generally, with assignments for theme anthologies. Usually if I come up with an idea at all, it's several years *after* the anthology has been published. I'll suddenly get a fabulous idea for a science fiction story about artichokes, but by then the artichoke anthology will be completed and turned in, so it doesn't do me any good. The irony in this case is that I actually *did* complete a story on time, and then they didn't *want* it.

At any rate, Ellen called me up and asked me to do a cat horror story. I sat and thought about it, and I scratched my head, and I thought about it some more. I couldn't muster up any real enthusiasm for this project. Because I'd read many cat horror story anthologies, and I knew that what was going to be true in ninety percent of the cases was that the cat would turn out to be a vampire, or would rip somebody's throat out, or would be a monster or a demon or something, or the Devil in disguise.

I couldn't muster up any enthusiasm for this. Not only because I had seen these type of stories again and again and again in the horror anthologies and semi-prozines, but also because I *like* cats! I've always been a cat person, I like cats, and I didn't particularly want to write a story in which...

You've owned several hundred of them yourself.

Gardner Dozois: I've owned several hundred of them, yes. Or so it sometimes seems. I didn't want to write a story in which cats were demons or vampires or something. That didn't appeal to me. So I started playing with the assignment, and I said, "Well, what would a horror story be like to a *cat?* If a cat were telling a horror story, what would that be like?" That seemed more interesting to me, and it gave me a glimmer of an idea. So I sat down and began writing the kind of horror story that cats would tell each other around a campfire, if they went to a summer camp for cats and told each other campfire Hook-Man type horror stories. I tried to think what would be horrible to a cat? What would horrify and scare them? What would the world look like from their perspective if they had intelligence enough to understand all of these things?

So I went around asking people to tell me horrible things that had happened to their cats. I believe it was you, Michael, who told me the story of the cat going up inside the hood of the car and getting chopped up when the guy started the car the next day.

We got the cat out before that happened. We went next door, and said, "Frank, would you pop your hood? Our cat is inside your engine." He clearly thought we were mad, but being a neighbor was too polite to say so, and went out and did so. He was, of course, shaken by the thought of what it could have been like the next morning when he started his car.

Gardner Dozois: And, indeed, I have heard from other people subsequently that this sort of thing actually *does* happen.

I have to say that I'm annoyed that you threw in the names of the cats of all of our friends except us. ***Our*** **cat, Shadowfax, didn't get his name into the story.**

Gardner Dozois: I did throw in the name of Greg Frost's cat, Pooter, who was still alive at the time, and several of our old, dead cats are in there. (They were alive when we *had* them, I should add!)

Mainly what the story is is just looking at life from a cat's perspective and trying to figure out what *they* would find to be a fit subject for a horror story. It seems to me it would be things like being run over by cars. And especially going to the vet. Cats don't really understand about going to the vet. They call it the Pain Place in the story. Which seems to me perfectly logical, that they would call it that. From the cat's perspective, their humans wait until they feel really sick and then drag them to this place where they're prodded and have things stuck up their ass and have their blood sucked out. The humans are really mean to wait until they really feel sick, and then subject them to this torture.

The incident where the cat is put to sleep while the humans stand around and pat it and talk to it is taken from my own experience. We had that happen with a beloved cat of ours that we had to put down. We stood around her and patted her while ostensibly she was put easily and painlessly to sleep. It turned out, to the embarrassment of the veterinarian, that it didn't work, and he had to keep upping the dosage and upping the dosage and she still had not died. We're patting her and saying, "Oh, it'll be all right," and all the other insincere, meaningless things that you say. Of course, she did eventually die. But this was a horrific thing to go through. Everybody, including the vet, was in tears by the time the poor cat finally died. It just struck me how this would look to another cat in the other room. It wouldn't look good.

Of course the old rogue is basically right, though he's putting his own twist on things. No matter how good you are as a cat, and you like your humans and you think they love you, eventually, if you live long enough, they're going to take you to the Pain Place and have you put down. They're going to *kill* you. So from his own perspective, he's perfectly right, no matter how the humans see it.

I also tried to work in the supernatural life of the cats, which I figured would be on a rather primitive, tribal level. They would see the planes in the sky overhead with their lights on as they descended toward the airport to land, and how could the cats possibly know what those were? They'd be just enormous monsters roaring through the sky with a blazing light. They would be demons of some sort, obviously.

Cars would also be puzzling to cats, I would think. They're not alive, the cats can *smell* that they're not alive. And yet, they run over you and kill you! Which would seem like a monstrous supernatural horror to a cat, I would imagine.

There's a legend in there that the People, as the cats call themselves, will outlive humans, and that this plague of civilization will just go painlessly away, and they'll return to Eden, which I kind of liked.

Gardner Dozois: I wrote the cats as a kind of tribal people, which is why they call themselves the People, of course. Obviously they don't write anything down, so they have a rich oral tradition, and all sorts of legends and superstitions. There's a cat ghost story embedded in the tale, told from the perspective of a cat. One of the cats grows quite wild-eyed about having seen the ghost of his dead house-mate outside scratching at the door, wanting to come in. That seemed appropriate to me.

I think it's a fun story. I had more fun with it than I usually do with stories. I allowed myself several arch indulgences, such as putting in footnotes which, in pseudo-scholarly terms, explain various things about the culture and language of the cats.

I thought it was a pretty good story, in fact, as cat stories go. But I found, when I delivered it to Ellen's cat anthology, that she didn't like it at *all*. She hated it, in fact, and rejected it. So there I was, having written this cat horror story, which Ellen didn't like because it didn't have vampire cats or demon cats in it, and so I was stuck with it. So I cast around for what to do with it, and I sent it to F&SF.

Of course Kris Rusch is also a cat-lover, and I thought she might appreciate it. And she bought it. And the rest is history. The Pulitzer Prize, the cheering crowds of millions, the dead cats sent to me in plastic bags...the list goes on and on!

"About ten p.m., I go out front and borrow my husband's pick-up truck. Henry stays behind watching TV, of course. He has a bad leg, and besides, he has no stomach for this sort of work. Which is okay, the Lord made different kinds of people for different kinds of work, I guess, and I'm content to do what it's been put in front of my hand to do, and not worry about whether other people have been called to do the same thing or not."

"Community" appeared in the September, 1996 issue of ASIMOV'S SCIENCE FICTION, Sheila Williams acting as purchaser for this one. This is a dark and yet relatively simple story. A woman, a minister, goes out with a batch of the boys on an "intervention." As is by now a common pattern,

the reader doesn't find out what's going on until midway through the story.

Gardner Dozois: This is why Stephen King trembles in his boots at the thought of me pushing him off the best-seller list.

How did this one get started?

Gardner Dozois: This is one of those stories that is entirely dependent on the voice of the narrator. I started hearing the voice of the narrator speaking key phrases of the story in my head and I wrote down the key sections in her voice. Then, once I had gotten that all down, I wrote up the narrative structure around it, and filled in. But it was voice of the narrative character that was important here.

This has happened once or twice before. Large sections of "Disciples" were like that, and chunks of "Flash Point." Once I could hear the character's voice speaking clearly in my head, I could write down things the way he would have phrased them. It was the same here. That's what really carried the story. The way the narrator *says* things, in the way that she would say them and nobody else would say them.

As far as what started me thinking about this incredibly unsympathetic character in the first place, I was watching some sort of smug TV show—it could have been Oprah or Jerry Springer, some kind of show of that ilk—where they were talking very self-satisfiedly about doing interventions. They were even, I believe, talking about interventions to keep people from smoking. They were being very smug and self-satisfied about all of this, and that irked me. I began thinking about the whole idea of intervening in a person's life to make it a better life, from your perspective, and by your values, and how everything you're doing is for their own good, and they'll thank you for it when they come to their senses, and so on and so forth. And the same day that I was listening to this Jerry Springer-like show, there was also an item on the news about an old woman somewhere near Philadelphia who had had dozens of cats in her house. Somebody had finally called the police, and they came in and they caged up all of her cats and took them away, while she protested futilely. That seemed to fit in with the "intervention" stuff, so that went into the mix too.

So all of this intervention stuff struck me as smug and self-satisfied and smarmy, and also a very dangerous kind of attitude to adopt. Because eventually it would lead to being able to justify almost *anything* you did to make people live the way *you* wanted them to live instead of the way *they* wanted to live.

So I was looking at this from a disapproving, critical perspective anyway. The character I started thinking about was one of these self-satisfied people who never sees the negative implications of her own actions, and is really sort of blind and immune to any self-criticism. She *knows* that what she's doing is right, and so she can do anything that she wants to, no matter how morally hideous it is.

Once I started thinking about this in these terms, I got the character, and then I began hearing the key phrasings in the story speaking themselves in my head. I scribbled them down. Then it was merely a matter of rationalizing them into some kind of coherent structure, and coming up with at least a bit of a snapper ending.

The whole thing only took about an afternoon, as I recall. By the time evening came, I was pretty much through with the story. It certainly couldn't sustain a lot more length. It's not an idea that you could stretch out to any great length. It had to be short and concise to have any real impact.

The last line of the story, in the woman's voice, is "What goes around, *comes* around." The implication there is that she'll get her comeuppance one of these days, but has no awareness of this.

Gardner Dozois: I sort of liked that, in that she's speaking the line that indicates that she's going to get her *own* comeuppance, and is not even aware of the irony of what she's saying. The major problem with the crafting of the story was how to get across at the end that she *was* going to get her comeuppance, without being really obvious about it—having her shot, or dragged off shrieking into the bushes to be crucified or something. I didn't want to go that route. I wanted to *imply* the ending that I thought was going to eventually happen without actually coming out and showing it. I particularly liked being able to have her say it in her own snippy, self-satisfied voice, because she obviously doesn't have a clue that one of these nights the one that they're coming after is going to be *her.*

Another way that I tried to set this up was by having little elements of tension within the group of interventionists that she's aware of but doesn't give enough weight to.

She's aware that Josh, for example, would just as soon rape the woman on the way out and is annoyed that she won't let him.

Gardner Dozois: And the whole business where Josh sits in the front seat against her wishes, and she has to glare him back into going into the back seat. There are other little murmurs of rebelliousness that, again, she notices but doesn't draw the correct conclusions from. I thought I had maybe gone a bit over the top, but felt it was necessary to make the ending make sense, where I had one of the men mutter ominously to her that her own husband had been drinking quite a bit. Which really ought to tip her off. But, again, because of her arrogance and self-satisfaction, she's oblivious to the real implications of this remark. And I wondered if maybe that was foreshadowing too much, making it a little too obvious...but I finally decided to let it stand, because I felt that without it there was a danger that people would miss the irony of what she's saying at the end.

You can't be too subtle with a genre audience. They're not big on nuance.

Gardner Dozois: Well, that's true. Irony is not something that the genre audience *gets* to a large extent, as I've discovered over the years. If you have a character say something or do something ironically, the chances are good that a high percentage of the reading audience is going to take you at face value. So you have to be careful with irony in this field. It's not a highly valued or highly understood part of the tool box. You always run the risk of having people think that the ironic statements that you have coming out of your characters' mouths are your *own* deeply cherished beliefs.

So I tried to convey through the tone that I didn't *really* think myself that it was all that good an idea to break into people's houses and beat their cat to death with baseball bats because they had too many cats, or to come in and kill their son because he has heavy metal posters on the wall. Because many people will think you *are* endorsing such stuff, just by showing it happening.

I will say, although this may seem like an obvious if-this-goes-on type of thing to some critics, that there *have* been times when the country has been dangerously close to creating an atmosphere where you could actually *do* these sorts of things. Back in the tag end of the Reagan years, when the Religious Right was really getting strong, we were skating close to an atmosphere where you could get away with doing stuff like this. So it's perhaps not quite as obvious as it might seem, to warn that if these trends go on, we could end up in this particular social position. Even today, there are people who would do *all* of these things, if they had the power to do so, I have no doubt of that.

"Like all intelligent creatures, it adapted."

Now we come to "Ancestral Voices," which I think is a nifty story. It was co-written with me, and appeared in the August 1998 issue of ASIMOV'S SCIENCE FICTION. I particularly liked the very opening, which is seen from the viewpoint of the alien, running in terror across the rooftops of Center City, Philadelphia. How did you come to write that, and when?

Gardner Dozois: I started this story back sometime in the early eighties, when we were in our Fiction Factory phase, and we were all writing collaborative stories such as "The Gods of Mars" and "Touring" and "Golden Apples of the Sun" and "Down Among the Dead Men." We were writing a lot, then.

I was writing a lot of solo stories too. When I started this particular story, I don't think I meant it to be a collaboration. I wrote the opening part pretty much the way it is on the page, where you see things from the perspective of the alien, then you see a bit about the alien in Philadelphia. That everything is seen from the perspective of the alien is what fueled the early part of the story creatively. I really enjoyed that, coming up with the alien perspective on the everyday world. I believe I carried the story through to the scene where the alien is nailed up in a dresser drawer.

Yeah, just a little bit before it was shipped off to Vermont.

Gardner Dozois: At that point I ran dry on it. Part of the problem with the story was, I could see that you'd have to have a situation in Vermont where you'd have a classic trapped-in-a-house-with-a-monster scenario: a large cast of characters, lots of cannon fodder, the alien killing them off, and them trying to protect themselves against the alien. Although I always intended for part of it to be from the alien's point of view, in which *they're* the monsters and not him. I wanted there to be an ironic balance.

From an early period, I got the idea of an old woman and her child. I don't think I specified the sex of the child. But I knew that what I wanted to do was have the child be killed and the old woman able to kill the monster but deciding not to because she realizes at the end, when it regains its senses, that it was an alien ambassador. So all that was in place.

You assured me that you *could* write this ending. I was reluctant to get into it because there's an iron law of writing that if you kill a child in a story, the reader will not forgive you for it. I told you that if I got involved, you'd have to write the ending. I couldn't possibly come up with a conclusion that would make the reader accept the child's death.

Gardner Dozois: I worked on this for a while in the early eighties, and sometime in the mid-eighties, I invited you to do this as a collaboration. I had given up on doing it as a solo story by then. And it sort of sat there, for years and years. You did a version that brought it up through some of the events in the house in Vermont. We ran it through a Philford workshop in '86, I think, so you had worked on it by then. But there was no ending.

It would lie fallow for a couple of years at a time, and then I would pick it up or you would pick it up, and move it along.

Mostly the story required big doses of manipulation. Someone would cry, "Don't go into the cellar!" and the other person would say, "No, no, I'm going down!" and the

first person would say, "No! Don't! You'll be eaten!"and the second would say, "No, I'm going down in the cellar with my flashlight!" Endlessly. We worked that for all it was worth.

Gardner Dozois: It was even more postmodern than that. Because they're saying, "Don't go down there in the cellar with a flashlight, because it'll be just like a monster movie where somebody goes down in the cellar with a flashlight and gets eaten!" And then he goes down into the cellar with his flashlight *anyway,* even though he *knows* what happens to people in monster movies.

People never learn. I wrote a scene where the old woman goes out in the cold to retrieve the battery from the car, and her fingers are crippled with arthritis so it's a hellishly difficult task for her to accomplish. It's described in excruciating detail, and then, when with great effort and ingenuity she breaks the battery out of the car, she can't lift it off the ground, so the problem starts all over again. I got enormous satisfaction from the sheer shamelessness of it. I could feel the reader writhing in agony. It was a scene that really milked the moose!

Gardner Dozois: This is called writing suspense. This is what you have to do when you're trying to engender fear for the characters in the reader.

I enjoyed it, but I couldn't respect it.

Gardner Dozois: I believe there were two problems that stalled this story for years. One was that we needed to think up a good clever, high-tech ANALOG-writer-like way for her to defend herself against the monster and ultimately defeat it. I was out of my depth there. I had no idea how she could do this. I'm sure a real ANALOG writer could have whipped up one in five minutes, in between turns on the exercise bike, but we had a lot more difficulty.

The other problem was, emotionally, how did you bring off the ending that I wanted? Where it had killed everybody she knew, and yet she would decide *not* to kill it when she had the chance. How do you make that emotionally credible to the reader? And in a way that will not cause him to throw the magazine down in disgust?

I finally got it written all the way to the ending and returned it to you, and you took a couple of years getting around to writing it. It was very frustrating because I couldn't go to you and say, "Look, Gardner, I got this thing to you in eight years, and now you've been holding onto it for two..."

Gardner Dozois: It's a good thing we didn't set out to write the novel version. We would still be grinding on into the twenty-first century.

Actually, I believe we discussed this possibility briefly at one point. It would have been fairly easy to make this into a novel, just by plugging more cannon fodder into the story.

Instead of it being a farmhouse, it would've been a community theater that was snowed in.

Gardner Dozois: I believe that was what we discussed. A community theater where they'd be doing a production of *Othello* in her barn. They'd all be trapped by the snowstorm, and this would give them plenty of opportunity to be killed by the alien, one by one.

We probably would have had to come up with another way for the monster to be defeated. You'd have to have it be defeated *one* way, and then it figures out a counter, and then you have to figure out *another* way to defeat it. Just having it happen the way it does in the story wouldn't be sufficient.

I think that this could have been turned into a novel. It wouldn't have been a particularly *good* novel. But it quite probably could have been sold, at the time, anyway, and it would be no worse than any number of other novels of this sort.

Let's see if we can figure out who contributed what characters. I know that the old woman was mine, because it was based on a small incident when I was working as a yard man. This very aristocratic woman was telling me exactly how she wanted me to perform the chores in her yard, in excruciating detail. But when she tried to show me the right way to tie up the trash bags after I'd picked up the yard litter, her hand froze up with arthritis and she couldn't tie the little twists. Her eyes filled up with tears and she flung the bag down, and said, "Oh, *you* do it!" and fled into the house. That was my vision of the character, that she had this great dignity and prickly sense of pride.

Gardner Dozois: I'm sure that the bulk of the human characters were yours. I had the idea of it being sent to an isolated farm where the monster could then run around and eat everybody and they wouldn't be able to escape, and so on and so forth. But once that was in place as a given, the character of the protagonist was yours.

This choice may have been influenced to some degree by the random chance that I had written down that it was being sent off to Vermont. If we had written down that it was being shipped to New Mexico instead, we might have come up with a different character.

But, no, I'm pretty sure that most of the human characters are yours. You certainly came up with the father and his road-house pickup girlfriend. Those were yours as well. I added a little bit of retro-characterization after the fact, on Alma, in that I threw in a couple of things about her past that you had not spelled out particularly, like her daughter being killed in a terrorist explosion and the fact that her father had been killed in World War Two. I put those little bits in to build her character in a certain direction that I thought would be useful for the story. But essentially, the characterization was yours.

Those bits also lead directly to the moral center of the story's ending, since they demonstrate that there's a real need for improvement in the human condition, which the alien potentially can provide.

Gardner Dozois: That was the one way which I finally saw to get around my self-imposed problem with the story, which is how do you make it credible that she'd have the creature in her power and *not* kill it, even though it killed her granddaughter. The only way I could see that it might be believable that she wouldn't kill the alien was if you had established already in the story that she had this really deep moral revulsion toward war that went back for generations, because she felt war had pretty much blighted her life and was going to go on and on like this, blighting people's lives forever in the future—and she came to believe that the alien might be able to bring a permanent peace to Earth. Which is why I introduced the little snippet of a scene where she's listening to the radio in the kitchen and it's talking about the next war which they're building up for. The idea being that one of the few things that could make her let the creature go would be if it could obliquely promise her it could do away with war. Then maybe she could rationalize it to herself that letting it live would save *other* people's children.

Even so, I don't think it would be at all realistic except for the fact that, having *done* the "right thing," we then show her being very bitter about it, and regretting that she hadn't done the wrong thing instead rather than the moral thing. But it was just enough of a rationalization that I thought we could make it believable on the page, in the instant that you were reading it, that those moral considerations might be enough to talk her into forgoing her revenge and letting the creature live. Especially as stressed-out and exhausted as she was.

Having written the bulk of the second section, at least the first draft of it, I think I can say without a great deal of offense that most of that doesn't interest me terribly. It's just hard work and craftsmanship. The needs of a horror story are much less interesting than those of a science fiction or fantasy story, as far as I'm concerned. You have to keep things going, you have to keep the suspense simmering, you have to keep the people reasonably interesting and plausible, but there's not a lot happening other than the reader being carried along. So let's skip toward the end—

Gardner Dozois: Before you skip to the end, I'd like to throw in that one of the things that I was interested in doing with this story was writing a story that played fair with the reader, that played by the rules of a horror story, that did all of the things that a horror story was supposed to do, and yet could be inverted, with a twist of your head, like those pictures that look like either a crone or a young woman depending on which way you squint at them, that could be turned into being an actually valid science fiction story. It would not violate the rules either as a science fiction story or a horror story. It could be looked at as one or the other with equal validity. All of the horror would have a science fiction rationale, and all of the science fiction elements would be looked at in the esthetic way of horror.

The dual nature of the story was what really amused me. Which in fact is what many critics have criticized it the most severely for having, that dual nature. But that was what I was interested in. Because, as in fact I think I said earlier, from the *creature's* point of view, *it's* not the monster at all. The *humans* it encounters are the monsters. I wanted to maintain that double perspective throughout.

It was a very elegant creature, and in some way electrical in nature, or at least strongly influenced by electrical phenomenon. As I recall, that was what stalled us for all those years. We kept looking for a hard science fiction plausible way to fight it and possibly trap it, and at the end shock it back into sentience. Which we ultimately didn't find. But I ultimately came up with two ploys. I had the people countering the monster using hand-held calculators, which it sees as complex electrical patterns and fears, mistaking them for weapons. Then at the end, it's given an electrical shock, and that accomplishes everything that needs to be done. In retrospect it's hard to see what the big problem was. Yet it stalled me for years.

Gardner Dozois: I'm sure if we had been Steve Baxter or Greg Egan or someone, we could have solved this problem in an afternoon. But nevertheless, we did have difficulty with it.

There had to be some way not just to *kill* it—we probably could have thought of several ways to do that—but to incapacitate it in such a way that it would get its memory back *and* be at the mercy of the woman, who could then choose to kill it or not kill it.

That brings us up to the ending, which the reviewers all hated. "Whoah! What's this *science fiction* doing in our horror story?" They wanted a stock horror ending. Which wouldn't have been much fun to write.

Gardner Dozois: No, it wouldn't have had much impact on the reader either, I don't think.

There's only two things to do with this story if you were to write it as a stock horror story. Either she manages to triumph and kills it, the less common ending, or she *thinks* that she has defeated it, and then it springs up at the last possible moment and defeats her after all. Something like eighty percent of horror stories end like that. Frankly, that's what I *liked* about the ending, that it *wasn't* a horror ending. We pulled it out into a science fiction ending. That's where I wanted to go from the beginning. It would have been a hell of a lot easier to write the story if we just had it being about this ravening monster that couldn't be defeated and eats all the people in this farmhouse.

I suppose the reason this story took so long to write is my own fault. From the beginning, I insisted on this weird twist, where she would have the creature in her power and decide to let it live, even though it had done her grievous harm by killing her grandchild. That was one of the things that interested me about the story, that moral dilemma. And yet it certainly would have been enormously easier to write *without* any of those moral complications, simply because it was so hard to come up with a way to make it plausible on the page, while the reader was reading the story, that this woman would actually let a creature that had killed her grandchild live. I couldn't see a way to do that for a long time. That for me was the big stumbling block for the story. The fact that we needed some way to counter and incapacitate the creature without killing it, was relatively minor in my opinion, even though it also stalled us for years. But I thought you would figure out a way to do that eventually.

Figuring out a way to have the creature kill her grandchild and still make it credible that she would let it live was a much harder problem. The only way that I could finally see to solve it was, after you had done your final draft, I went in and added little interstitial snippets throughout the last part of the story that build up the idea of her lifelong hatred of and revulsion to war, and that the creature might be bringing peace to the Earth, something that might make it seem worthwhile to her to let it go at the end. That was the only way that I could see to make it work even in the slightest.

If it hadn't been for the moral difficulty of the ending, I

don't think either of us would have bothered doing all the work it took to write this novella.

Gardner Dozois: No, to me that's what makes the story worthwhile. Although, as you pointed out, some of the reviewers did not agree, and would have, I think, been happier with the story if it didn't have what at least one of them called a "tacked-on science fiction ending." Which I though was kind of amusing, because that "tacked-on ending" was the whole driving force behind the story's genesis in the first place.

For what it's worth, we workshopped this story in the Philford Workshop in '86, and it got pretty much torn up, as I recall. Pretty much nobody liked it. It wasn't all there, I should add, the whole ending section was not there yet. But everybody pretty much hated it, which should have braced us for the critical response we were going to get later.

Interestingly, what most of them hated was the fact that it was "a stock, generic horror story." Interesting to speculate whether any of them would have changed their minds and liked it better if we'd had the so-called "tacked-on science fiction ending" at that point. But we'll never know.

One neat touch here is that I *tell* you that the creature is intelligent in the very first line, and then spend the rest of the story slyly misdirecting you away from that realization.

"Sometimes the old man was visited by time travelers."

We now come to the last and final story you've ever written—

Gardner Dozois: Maybe true. At my age, you never know.

—as of today, at any rate. It's "A Knight of Ghosts and Shadows,' which appeared in the October/November 1999 issue of ASIMOV'S SCIENCE FICTION, and which I think is an interesting story from almost any aspect. Let's start at the very beginning. The first line, "Sometimes the old man was visited by time travelers," is very explicitly science fiction. It tells you straight out that there are time travelers. But then it's immediately followed by a careful description of the old man shambling through his house, focusing on how ordinary it is, and how old it is, and the dust and the old furniture, and you suggest that it may be senile dementia, that there aren't time travelers at all. You almost undercut that opening, but not quite. Then, after establishing the old man's life and character expressed through the setting, you give his name, Charles Czudak, say that he's eighty years old today, his eyes open, and you begin the story a second time in a different voice.

Gardner Dozois: Perhaps this is making a virtue of necessity. This is a story where I wrote the opening section somewhere around 1978, I think it was. The opening two or three pages were written in one sitting, and then I stalled on the story, pretty much at the place where it breaks.

Yeah, yeah, "His eyes opened," is where the real break is in the story.

I had originally written a page, maybe a page and a half, *after* that, but then the story stalled. It wasn't going anywhere. So I put the story aside, and then last year I was looking through old fragments for something that I could turn into a story, and it struck me that this was a perfectly serviceable opening. That it just needed to be taken somewhere different. So I threw away the page or so that I had written after the break, and started writing the new material.

The story was always going to go in a sort of similar direction to where it goes now. Even some of the elements were already in place in my head, like him meeting his ex-wife or -lover and she's now immortal and he's old. So some of the plot was already there. I think it again was a failure of imagination in some ways, in that I had difficulty, once Czudak went downstairs out of his bedroom, imagining what the world outside his house was going to *look* like.

Perhaps as a result of being an editor of ASIMOV'S and doing a best-of-the-year anthology and reading all these stories by Hot Young Turks of the nineties, I realized that the only way the story was going to work at all was to up the imagination ante considerably from the kind of semi-ruined post-apocalyptic society I had vaguely had in mind from the start. That was too seventies-ish. It had to be made richer and stranger and more numinous. So I just pulled out the stops and made it as bizarrely imaginative as I could possibly make it, without worrying about any logical inconsistencies or whether a society set up like this could actually *function* or not. As a result, I managed to pull off a sort of pale, feeble imitation of a story by somebody like Greg Egan, who actually *does* have an imagination. But at least it allowed me to go forward and bring the story to its conclusion.

Another element I think influenced the story was reading a book called *Digital Delirium*, which is a non-fiction book wherein many authors from within the field and beyond the field make outrageous claims about the effects that virtual reality is going to have on our society in the future. I found that the science fiction writers were far more restrained and reasonable about their predictions than most of the loony futurists were. Who were really imagining scenarios that struck me as complete bullshit.

So some of this is sort of a response to some of the more extreme speculative elements in that book. It probably is also a reflection of other things I've been reading in scientific news and nonfiction. This whole argument about the meat versus the transmogrification into the machine is another argument that's been fighting itself out back and forth in science fiction for the last couple of decades, with the tide of sentiment first swinging one way and then swinging the other. So I wanted to give my take on that issue.

Because of the way I had wanted the story to be structured from the start, I tried to make the best case I possibly could make for *both* sides of the proposition. In fact, for every idea that is raised in the story, I tried to make as good a case as I could for both sides of the argument. This of course leads down to the ending of the story, where the ending could go either one way or the other. What I worked hardest at in the story was crafting it so that there was nothing on the page that you could point at that would definitely say one way or the other which decision he was going to make. I wanted to funnel it down to the point right before the wave function collapses, where he still could potentially go either way.

It's like Schrödinger's Cat. By the time the story ends, you don't know whether the cat is alive or dead, it's sort of both. I deliberately wanted it to end before the wave function collapses, and it's pinned-down which decision he makes, which way the universe is going to split. A lot of conscious craft went into making sure that there were equally valid arguments for both ways that the story could go, so that there was no real way that the reader could tell which way was more likely.

This is another story, where instead of the standard model where somebody has a problem and the suspense comes from whether he'll solve it or not, something very strange is happening and the reader stays with the story to figure out what the heck is going on. I notice that as you go along you keep dropping more hints, some misleading—at one point Czudak figures out the time travelers have come to see him die, at which point the suspense comes from wondering whether he's going to die or not. But that's just

**misdirection. In fact, you have a careful string of hints and
misdirections all the way through the story.**

Gardner Dozois: You'll notice, by the way, that I also never
actually resolve the question of whether the time travelers are
real or just a subjective part of his imagination. That's never
resolved for certain either. That was also deliberate.

**Although in science fiction they are going to be read as
being real. Where if you'd published this in a literary journal, the presumption would be that they were signs of
dementia.**

Gardner Dozois: True. Of course, a literary journal wouldn't
have touched it with a forty-foot pole. But that's another matter.
  Yes, it's quite true that the expectations of genre weight it a
bit in one way, toward one interpretation, but my steadfast
refusal to admit that they're actually real—even at the end,
when he's ready to make this momentous decision, he's still not
sure whether there actually are time travelers there, or he's just
making the whole thing up—makes it as ambiguous as possible, given the fact that it was going to have to appear in a genre
magazine if it appeared anywhere at all.

**So after the opening, Czudak reflects back on the ther-
monuclear war, which I think reflects a break with seventies science fiction which would have thrown the story into
a post-apocalyptic setting. But now it's just another part of
history. "Well, we had a thermonuclear war, other stuff
happened, and now we have New Men and other strange
people living next door..."**

Gardner Dozois: That was again what I was trying to get across.
Life does go on, as long as we can dodge the dinosaur-killer
asteroid as a species. You get used to things quickly. I once lived

in Nuremberg, in Germany, which had been ninety percent destroyed during World War Two. You could go to the museum there and see the diorama of what it'd been like, with maybe one building left standing for miles. All the rest of the city just rubble. And yet by the time I got there, they had built it all back *up* again, looking just the way that it had before, and people were leading their daily lives and not paying much attention to the fact that the city they lived in had been leveled to the ground within the lifetime of most of the people living there. So it seems to me that that would probably be the same way it would be with thermonuclear war or any other such catastrophe. If humanity survived through it, it would be just an unimportant thing in the past within decades for most of the population. Everybody would just shrug and get on with their lives.

Czudak putters about in the kitchen and all of a sudden his virtual valet notifies him that he has calls. Which comes as a bit of a shock after the extremely mundane opening. From that point on, you just keep turning up the heat with more and more details, each one progressively weirder than the one before. Until you've got things like the Isolate next door—any number of people have gotten themselves merged into one biological entity which peers out the window to see what the weird neighbors are up to, and then goes back to his/her/their own life. It starts out being one kind of story and then it segues seamlessly into a very different one.

Gardner Dozois: Well, as I said, this was sort of making a virtue of necessity. The original story, though it had some of the same thematic elements, would have been a very seventies kind of story because, of course, I am an outdated, obsolete, seventies kind of a writer. This was my attempt to see if I could actually write a *nineties* sort of a story instead, and I think that I managed to turn in at least a feeble imitation of a nineties sort of a story. Of course, the real radical young kids are no doubt out there right now sneering at my feeble, senile efforts to write up-to-date fiction. "The old man is past it!"

But thematically, I think it works out well that it starts with him in a very limited, ordinary, mundane environment that could be taking place in any decade, and then slowly turns up the heat. I think you once made a comment in a writing workshop about how you boil the frog by slow degrees. That's sort of what I'm doing here. By the time the story is half over, I've dumped you into a future that probably will be strange and alien to most readers. And yet it starts with him in a much more mundane pot of water, which then becomes boiled by slow degrees as the story progresses.

The point where the valet comes in is the point where I really started to bite into the story. I was throwing away a lot of the stuff that I would have had him do in the story if I had written it in the seventies. Right away, you're jolting him into the nineties or thc aughts, because he has this electronic valet that speaks to him from the walls.

So, a rather mild bit of techno-shock, but one at least that starts the fuse smoldering to burn the story in the right direction.

You've got a large number of different kinds of things and particularly different kinds of people coexisting in the background.

Gardner Dozois: The people in the background of the story, the society in the background of the story, probably reflect a feeling that I've long had, which I think is similar to Vernor Vinge's "singularity" idea. Which is that if the rate of technological change progresses and continues to accelerate in the way that it's been accelerating, the people we would end up with in the future would be almost completely incomprehensible to us.

But at the same time, another thing that went in here is that I felt that high-tech future stories show the future society as being too *homogenous*. It is all the same kind of mind-set, all the same kind of lifestyles, from top to bottom. And that's not the way that society works, as far as I can see. Society is *layered*, like nougat. You have people living a sophisticated kind of existence in extremely high-tech urban cocoons, within a block of people sleeping in the park or on a hot air vent who are essentially living the life of a hunter-gatherer from a Stone Age society.

So one of the things I wanted to bring out here is that even in the future, where you have this incredible, singularity-like acceleration of change, to the point where some people are incomprehensible near-gods, in terms of their control of technology, you would also have people who would be living the same way they always did. You would have lots of different layers of society, and you would have lots of people reacting differently to the changes in society. Some would embrace them enthusiastically, and some would try to resist them, some would ignore the matter altogether, as far as they could, and just get on with their own lives.

Somewhere in here, thrown into the stew, is an idea that I once had, that doesn't get entirely expressed but is in the background meld somewhere, that we will eventually end up with *enclaves* in society that are frozen at different technological levels, different levels of sociological change, like we have now with the Amish and the Mennonites. Little enclaves of society where they decided to freeze themselves in 1990 and not go any further than that. "Okay, we'll have MTV, but we're not going to have personal teleporting machines!" Or freeze themselves in 1950, for that matter.

I think that's likely to happen to some degree, though they may not be formalized enclaves, or social groups as organized as the Amish. But you're going to have little pockets where it's effectively the nineteenth century, even though it's the twenty-second century.

It works that way right *here* and now, in the present. Within two hundred miles of here, there's probably somebody who doesn't have electricity. You go a thousand miles, and you'll probably find somebody who doesn't have indoor plumbing. While we live in our post-modern-beginning-of-the-twenty-first-century society, there are people in China or Mexico who are still living as subsistence-level dirt farmers, just as their ancestors have been living for thousands of years. It hasn't really changed much for them. What year is it for *them*?

So it's never turtles all the way down. There's always a stratification of society. This is something I try to get across in the background of the story, though it doesn't show up in the foreground all that much.

Czudak is approached by the AIs and offered immortality of a sort. I noticed that the characters urging him to take the offer, his ex-wife and Bucky Bug, the AI, are both drawn unsympathetically. So it's not just reasonable people saying to the old man, "Oh, come on, take your insulin so you won't die." It's a much harder thing for him to accept with his ex-wife there sneering at him.

Gardner Dozois: And yet, while she's sneering at him as a loser, I think I make it clear that there's still an undercurrent of affection there. I mean, she *wants* him to become an immortal, to some degree at least, you get the impression, so that they can be together again.

Also, I think a key fact here is the fact that she had tried to recruit him to join the ranks of the immortals in the first place, thirty years before, at some risk to her own position. So while there's a lot of Realpolitik going on here, it is also fueled under the surface to some degree by psychological factors. He and his ex-wife have a prickly sort of relationship. But it's clearly not a relationship that has actually *ended,* as far as the emotional context is concerned. Which, of course, is symbolized by the fact that even though he doesn't keep her picture up on the mantelpiece anymore, he obsessively keeps looking at the place where *her* picture had *been* on the mantelpiece.

It's also part of how I'm trying to make it valid that there would be a *decision* to be made here. That it's a *tough* decision for him. The real danger with the story is that it says, "Well, you can die and rot! Or we'll make you immortal and you can go to the stars!" And, if not presented entirely right, this may not seem like much of a *choice* or a moral dilemma to most people! But in order for the story to function the way I wanted it to function, with there being no real way to tell what decision he's going to make, the choice had to be presented in such a way that it seems feasible that he might actually turn it down.

Now, the fact that it's being presented by his ex-wife, in at least a superficially sneering way, and that there's all this history behind them, and all of this emotionality between them, both positive and negative, lends some credence to the idea that he might turn it down just because his *pride* has been injured. He's festered, he's brooded about this all these decades. It's conceivable that he might turn it down out of pride and hurt feelings just *because* his ex-wife is offering it to him. That's at least emotionally conceivable. In addition to him turning it down for all the idealistic, political, philosophical reasons.

And I will say, although some people probably won't believe this, that I have met a few people who probably *would*, under the same circumstances, turn this offer down.

As to which side of the argument *I* am on, I deliberately tried to obscure that. However, I think that if someone came and made this offer to *me* (which no one is actually going to *do*, more's the pity!), I would accept it in a hot second. Probably, Czudak does too. But I deliberately set it up so there's no way you can tell for sure.

The first however many times I read this, I thought it was left uncertain. But rereading the story for this interview, I noticed the lines just before the "Lady or the Tiger" final snapper line, are "Exultation opened hotly inside him like a wound. God, he loved the world! God, he loved life!" I can-

not but conclude that that was you peeking out from behind the character's mask there.

Gardner Dozois: I put that in to sort of give a hint, a subtle indication that he would choose being alive, rather than choose being morally superior and correct and dead. But, again, I tried not to pin it down. And I think you could still argue an ending where he turns them down anyway, and does it ringingly in prime time in front of an audience of millions.

I'm not sure *why* exactly, but it seemed important to me that you not be able to really tell which decision he was going to make. You can formulate your own theory and make a case for it. But there would be an equally valid, or nearly as valid, anyway, argument to be made for some *other* theory as to how the story was going to come out.

Perhaps it's all this collapsing-wave-function stuff that people have been talking about in the last couple of decades, but it seems to me that in life you never really *do* know the consequences of your actions or decisions. This was another thing that was in the back of my mind when I wrote this story. I had been thinking about how impossible time travel would be, because you would never know whether the things you were choosing were making things better or making things worse. You don't get on the plane and it crashes, so you're saved. But maybe on the way home from the airport, you're run over by a bus. There's no way to ever predict the consequences of your actions. If you decide to stay in the house today, maybe that saves your life because you don't get shot down the block. But, on the other hand, maybe a gas leak blows the house up, and you'd have been fine if you *had* gone out.

So you never know what the consequences of your decisions are going to be. I think that's built into the universe. Even the Zen answer of "Take no action, do nothing," doesn't get around this, because it could be that by taking no action and doing nothing, you are producing the undesirable outcome. So there really is no way around this particular dilemma, as far as I can see. You can never predict the outcome of any action. You can never really tell where anything is going to lead. You can't outguess the universe. You just have to throw the dice and take your chances.

That pretty much wraps it up. I thank you.

Gardner Dozois: You're welcome. You realize that you have just pulled off one of those completely useless but impressive accomplishments, like making a replica of the Titanic out of marzipan, or building the Eiffel Tower life-sized out of old used Q-tips.

Well, I always wanted to do something of that sort.

Gardner Dozois: I figure there's about five people in the world who are going to want to read this book. Maybe that's over-estimating it. But for what it's worth, you have done it.

For those Swanwick fans out there who would like to berate me for getting Michael to waste all this time doing this interview, when he could have more profitably spent the time writing novels and short stories instead, I tried to tell him not to bother, but he wouldn't listen to *me*.

It's strange looking back at your career in retrospect like this. It seems like it all shouldn't have taken anywhere near as long as it did. Damon Knight made a very similar remark to me once, after I'd written a critical retrospective of his career, and I understand what he meant much better now. There were really only three or four stories of mine that had any impact on the evolution of the field, and if you add up all the writing-time, I could have written them all in a month. The rest of my career I could have phoned in, and kicked back and put my feet up.

A Bibliography of First Publications

"Afternoon at Schrafft's", with Michael Swanwick & Jack Dann, AMAZING STORIES, March 1984.

"Ancestral Voices", with Michael Swanwick, ASIMOV'S SCIENCE FICTION, August 1998.

"Apres Moi", OMNI, November 1990.

"A Cat Horror Story," THE MAGAZINE OF FANTASY AND SCIENCE FICTION, November, 1994.

"Chains of the Sea", *Chains of the Sea*, ed. Robert Silverberg, Nelson, 1973.

"A Change in the Weather", PLAYBOY, June 1981.

"The City of God", with Michael Swanwick, OMNI ONLINE, 1995. First print publication: ASIMOV'S SCIENCE FICTION, October/November 1996.

"The Clowns", with Susan Casper & Jack Dann, PLAYBOY, August 1985.

"Community", Asimov's Science Fiction, September 1996.

"Conditioned Reflex", *Generation*, ed. David Gerrold, Dell, 1972.

"Disciples", PENTHOUSE, December 1981.

"Dinner Party", *Light Years and Dark*, ed. Michael Bishop, NY: Berkley, 1984.

"Down Among the Dead Men", with Jack Dann, OUI, July 1982

"A Dream at Noonday", *Orbit 7*, ed. Damon Knight, G.P. Putnam's, 1970.

"The Empty Man", WORLDS OF IF, September 1966.

"Executive Clemency", OMNI, November 1981.

"Flash Point", *Orbit 13*, ed. Damon Knight, G.P. Putnam's, 1974.

"Flying", EDGE, SF Directions, Autumn/Winter, 1973.

"The Gods of Mars", with Michael Swanwick & Jack Dann, OMNI, March 1985.

"Golden Apples of the Sun" (as "Virgin Territory"), with Michael Swanwick & Jack Dann, PENTHOUSE, March 1984.

"Horse of Air", *Orbit 8*, ed. Damon Knight, G.P. Putnam's, 1970.

"In a Crooked Year", *Ten Tomorrows*, ed. Roger Elwood, Fawcett, 1973.

"King Harvest", *New Dimensions 2*, ed. Robert Silverberg, NY: Doubleday, 1972.

"A Kingdom by the Sea", *Orbit 10*, ed. Damon Knight, G.P. Putnam's, 1972.

"A Knight of Ghosts and Shadows", ASIMOV'S SCIENCE FICTION, October/November 1999.

"The Last Day of July", *New Dimensions 3*, ed. Robert Silverberg, NY: Nelson Doubleday, 1973.

"Machines of Loving Grace", *Orbit 11*, ed. Damon Knight, G.P. Putnam's, 1972.

"The Man Who Waved Hello", *Universe 2*, ed. Terry Carr, NY: Ace, 1972.

"The Mayan Variation" AMAZING, September 1984.

"Morning Child", OMNI, January 1984.

Nightmare Blue, with George Alec Effinger, NY: Berkley, 1975.

"One for the Road", PLAYBOY, April 1982.

"Passage", *Xanadu*, ed. Jane Yolen, NY: Tor, 1993.

"The Peacemaker", ISAAC ASIMOV'S SCIENCE FICTION MAGAZINE, August 1983.

"Playing the Game", with Jack Dann, ROD SERLING'S THE TWILIGHT ZONE MAGAZINE, February 1981.

"The Sacrifice", THE MAGAZINE OF FANTASY AND SCIENCE FICTION, March 1982.

"Send No Money", with Susan Casper, ISAAC ASIMOV'S SCIENCE FICTION MAGAZINE, Mid-December 1985.

"Slow Dancing With Jesus", w/Jack Dann, PENTHOUSE, July 1983.

"Snow Job", with Michael Swanwick, HIGH TIMES, April 1982.

"Solace", OMNI, February 1990.

"The Sound of Muzak", *Quark 1*, ed. Samuel R. Delany and Marilyn Hacker, Paperback Library, 1970.

"A Special Kind of Morning", *New Dimensions I*, ed. Robert Silverberg, NY: Doubleday, 1971.

"The Storm", *Future Corruption*, ed. Roger Elwood, Warner, 1975.

"Strangers", *New Dimensions IV*, ed. Robert Silverberg, Signet, 1974.

Strangers, NY: Berkley/Putnam, 1978.

"The Stray", with Susan Casper, ROD SERLING'S THE TWILIGHT ZONE MAGAZINE, December 1987.

"Time Bride" with Jack Dann, PLAYBOY, December, 1983.

"Touring", with Jack Dann & Michael Swanwick, PENT-HOUSE, April 1981.

"A Traveler in an Antique Land", *Chrysalis 10*, ed. Roy Torgeson,NY: Doubleday,1983.

"The Visible Man", ANALOG, December 1975.

"Where No Sun Shines", *Orbit 6*, ed. Damon Knight, G.P. Putnam's, 1970.

"Wires", FANTASTIC, December 1971.

The Fiction of James Tiptree, Jr., nonfiction chapbook, NY: Algol Press, 1977.